Recipes from the
Vegetarian Hindu Cu[isine]

flavors of India

toor DAL P. 122

by Shanta Nimbark Sacharoff

Drawings by Linda Robertson

101 Productions   San Francisco   1972

Distributed to the book trade in the United States
by Charles Scribner's Sons, New York.

Library of Congress Catalog Card Number 79-182418

Sixth Printing, May 1981

PUBLISHED BY 101 PRODUCTIONS
834 Mission Street
San Francisco, California 94103

Preface

Western man has sought the riches of Indian spices for centuries. And Indians have cultivated the art of cooking meatless cuisine for more than twice that amount of time. It seems only natural that if a person has a high regard for life he will pay close attention to the food that he eats. I remember meeting my wife's father for the first time. We spoke of many things, but at one point he thought for a moment and asked me, "If man can live well by eating fruits, grains, vegetables and dairy products, why does he kill animals?" I was stuck for an answer. In my mind all I could think of was that it was for reasons of taste. But at that moment, speaking to this simple and wise old man, and knowing of his reverence for animal life, my answer seemed quite unsatisfactory. For the first time I realized how desensitized I had become to the taking of animal life. It was soon after this that I became a vegetarian. My wife, realizing that I was not familiar with Indian vegetarian cooking, was prepared to cook in whatever manner suited me. But she was very pleased by my decision not to eat meat. The reward for making this decision was the gift of Indian cooking. A gift that has no limits, a gift that never ceases to amaze me.

Stanley Sacharoff

west Gujarat State

TO MY FATHER

Contents

Introduction

There are hundreds of millions of vegetarians in this world. This would include the people of the non-meat eating religions such as the Hindus, Buddhists and Jains plus many others who respect and honor animal life. There are also many people who cannot afford to eat meat or do not have the means to preserve meat and for those reasons sustain vegetarian diets. The Hindu religion teaches its people to love and respect animal life, especially that of the cow who is very much of a mother earth figure to many Hindus. It is certainly a divine being that can eat grass and then produce life giving milk. Secondly, India is an agrarian country where most of the farming is done by bullock labor and therefore cows become more important as milk-giving and bull-producing living animals than as dietary items.

It is a well known story in India that when Ghandi, as a young man, went to England to study law, his mother made him promise that he would never touch wine, women or meat. Indians have been vegetarians for a great many years and because they have placed such great emphasis upon their vegetarianism, they have evolved a diet that is highly varied as well as nutritious and extremely tasteful. Those people who have eaten Indian food only in restaurants may not wholly agree to this point. Because, as I have found, most restaurants serving Indian food in the United States offer a poor substitute for the real thing. Only in London have I eaten in Indian restaurants that served food worthy of an Indian household. Even in India it is difficult to find a high-quality restaurant. The reason for this is that Indians are culturally not restaurant-going people. They do not have the time nor the money to entertain themselves in restaurants. In India if you find a friend eating in a restaurant you can usually assume that his wife is in the hospital delivering a baby. The women of India almost never get to eat in a restaurant.

In most of the Indian restaurants in America and even in India, there is a tendency to overspice the food. While it is true that Indian food is highly flavored with spices, it is nevertheless wrong to drown the taste of the food with the taste or hotness of the spices. In India, food with too much spice is considered *"tamasi"* and *"rajasi"* (aggressive) food, and it is written in the Hindu epics that this food is not desirable because it leads to aggressive behavior. The food cooked with the right amount of spices is called *"satvik"* (nutritious) food and is supposed to lead one towards calmness and good health.

In America, women usually know how to cook vegetables only one or two ways, resulting in food that is sometimes overcooked and lacking in taste. Boiling or overcooking not only takes away the taste but also the nutritional value of the food. Since in India a young girl is not considered a woman until she masters the art of cooking rice at least fifteen different ways, Indian women pride themselves on being able to create a tasty and well-balanced vegetarian menu.

A lack of satisfying tastes and concern over nutritional values are the reasons why people in the West find it difficult to sustain a vegetarian diet. They believe that there is a lack of proteins in a non-meat diet. This, of course, is not true. A diet rich in dry vegetables such as pulse (lentils) and *dals* (split grains), and containing a good supply of nut meats, milk and milk products would more than provide a person with enough proteins for the growth and sustenance of a healthy body.

This book then tries to contain all you would want to know about Indian vegetarian cooking and more. In India my family was always pleased by the subtle flavors of their food and here I have met many American friends who are concerned over the nutritional quality of their food. Therefore I have tried to combine the basically traditional Indian dishes with an evaluation of nutritional values and a bit of my own imagination, which is what cooking is all about. The recipes have innumerable virtues; mainly they are nutritious, inexpensive and delicious!

Spices

It is not the custom in India to put salt and pepper on the table when serving meals. In fact this would be considered an insult to the person preparing the food. When you are served Indian cuisine it is presumed that all the dishes are flavored with the right amount of spices. The art of blending flavors is an important prerequisite to the technique of Indian cooking.

You may be surprised to learn that women in India do not cook with curry powder. Curry powder is strictly a packaged item for western cooks who may be unfamiliar with the varying subtleties of different blends and combinations of Indian spices. As a mixture, curry powder serves as a poor substitute for individual ingredients. Therefore if you want to do a complete job when preparing an Indian meal, I would suggest you obtain at least these basic spices—turmeric powder, black mustard seeds, coriander powder, cumin powder, fresh garlic and cayenne powder. Many of these spices are common to other styles of cooking and all of them retain their flavors for quite a long time. Except

for the fresh garlic all the above mentioned spices should be stored in tightly sealed containers. Garlic stays longest when left out in the open or at least in an open jar.

In the following pages I will try and acquaint you with the different properties and qualities of spices used in Indian cooking. Sometimes certain spices are not available in particular areas. All the spices that I mention, however, can be obtained through mail-order spice emporiums, some of which I have listed at the end of this book. Sometimes one spice flavor can be substituted for the flavor of an unavailable spice, other times spices that are not obtainable can be left out entirely without spoiling the taste of the dish being prepared. Where substitutions or deletions can be made, it will be indicated whenever possible in the recipes. The amount of spices listed in the recipes of this book may produce too "mild" a dish. Those people who like their food to be more sensational can, according to their tastes, add hotter spices such as cayenne, onions, hot green chilis, etc.

Spices

The English name of the following spices is followed by the Hindi name, description and usage.

ASAFETIDA (Hing)

Hing is obtained from the dried root resins of a particular East Indian plant. It is sold as a fine brown powder. *Used in sautéing certain vegetables hing has a definite but acquired taste and can be ommited from recipes if unavailable or not desired.*

CARDAMOM SEED (Ilaichi)

Cardamom, an exotic spice originally from Nepal, is sold as a white or green pod about the size of a pea. The small dark seeds are inside the pod. Like cinnamon and clove, cardamom is a "sweet" spice. *A costly spice that is used for special occasions, it is best used whole as a flavoring to tea or in certain sweet dishes. When used whole the pod should be removed before serving. In India it is believed that cardamom will help relieve the symptoms of a cold.*

CAYENNE (Mirchi)

A dark bright red powder made from dried, hot red pepper, not to be confused with other hot pepper mixtures. A good substitute for this spice is fresh green hot pepper. *This spice is the main source of hotness in Indian food and should be used with care. A large intake of this spice is supposed to lead one towards greater sexual activity.*

CINNAMON (Taj)

Cinnamon is the bark of a tree that is common to Ceylon. Much of the cinnamon sold here is actually *cinnamon cassia,* a slightly bitter substitute for the real spice which is both sweet and hot. *In recipes that call for a whole stick cinnamon, the stick should be removed before the meal is served.*

CLOVES (Laving)

This distinctly flavored spice is the dried flower bud of a certain tropical tree. *Cloves are used whole in Indian cooking and should be removed before eating.*

CORIANDER (Dhania)

Fresh coriander looks like parsley and is also known as cilantro and Chinese parsley. Coriander powder is made from crushed coriander seeds which is a milder form of this strong tasting spice. *This popular Indian spice is usually available in stores serving Mexican or Chinese people. Coriander seeds can be ground in a pepper mill just before using to insure freshness. Fresh coriander is a source of protein.*

CUMIN (Jeera)

Cumin seeds look and smell somewhat like caraway seeds. This spice can be bought in powdered form that will hold its freshness for months. *An international spice that adds a special flavor to almost any vegetable.*

FENUGREEK SEEDS (Methi)

Fenugreek seeds are small and yellow. They have a slightly bitter but pleasant taste. *Fenugreek is said to aid one's digestion. If not available this spice can be omitted.*

GARLIC (Lasan)

Garlic powders or salts are not the same as fresh garlic. The outside skin of the individual pods should be removed. *Garlic has a number of medicinal uses and is prescribed in India as a cure for an acid stomach, among other things.*

GINGER ROOT (Adu)

These tough light brown roots are available in many ethnic grocery stores. The powdered form of ginger is a poor substitute for the strong pungent flavor of fresh ginger. *Ginger has a tendency to dry out in storage but can be revitalized by soaking in warm water. To chop the ginger finely, use small holes of a cheese grater.*

MINT (Phodino)

Fresh mint can be grown in a pot indoors or in a small space outside. The plant has a nice mint smell. *Used as a flavoring in hot or iced tea. An upset stomach can be soothed with a hot cup of mint tea.*

MUSTARD SEEDS (BLACK) (Rai)

These small black seeds are an essential part of Indian cooking, and are different in taste to the yellow mustard seeds. *Used in sautéing most vegetable and lentil dishes, this spice makes a characteristic sound when put in oil that allows the cook to know when the oil is ready.*

NUTMEG (Jaifal)

This spice is about the size of a walnut when whole and is available in powdered form in most stores. *Nutmeg is used most often as a topping for sweet milk dishes.*

PEPPER (Mari)

Not an often used spice in India, pepper tastes best when ground fresh from peppercorns. *A mild source of hotness used in salads and yogurt dishes.*

ROSE WATER (Gulab-jal)

An aromatic liquid made from crushed rose petals. *This essence is used mainly as a flavoring for sweet dishes and milk.*

Spices

SAFFRON *(Kesar)*

Saffron threads are the golden stigmas of a beautiful crocus plant that grows in India and in parts of Europe. *One of the most expensive spices in the world, saffron is used for a coloring agent as well as for the unique aroma it imparts to dishes. Saffron also has strong medicinal properties and should not be used in greater quantities than indicated.*

TAMARIND *(Imli)*

Another exotic spice, tamarind is a fruit resembling fresh peas in the pod. When ripe, tamarind possesses a sweet and sour taste. *This spice is sometimes available in stores in Spanish-speaking areas. If unavailable, this flavor can be simulated by a mixture of vinegar (or lemon) and brown sugar.*

TURMERIC *(Haldi)*

The poor man's saffron, turmeric is a most popular Indian spice used for its ability to color foods yellow as well as for its unique taste. Available whole as a root or ground this spice can be stored almost indefinitely. *An essential flavor to many Indian dishes. Turmeric taken fresh in root form is known to cure sore throats and back aches. Turmeric will not make a dish "hot."*

INGREDIENTS

I will try to list and describe some of the ingredients that are typical to Indian cooking but not so familiar to western cooks. All of the items mentioned are available through local grocery or speciality stores, or through the mail-order houses that I have listed at the back of this book.

CHICK-PEA FLOUR *(Besan)*

Chick-peas are heart-shaped yellow seeds that resemble peas. In India chick-peas are ground into a flour known as *besan.* Chick-pea flour not only makes good tasting dishes but is also a valuable source of protein. While not used as a daily menu item, chick-pea flour is reserved for the many delicacies that are prepared during the great number of holidays and festive occasions. Other nationalities in the West use a similar ingredient called garbanzo beans. Garbanzo beans are almost equal to chick-peas in taste and food value, and are more readily available. However, garbanzo flour is not so fine in texture as *besan.* When stored in a tightly sealed container, chick-pea flour can last for several months.

GARAM MASALA (HOT SPICE MIXTURE)

Although the combination of ingredients sometimes varies in different parts of India, *garam masala* is usually a mixture of cloves, cinnamon and cardamom seeds ground together in equal amounts. To prepare this mixture, first spread out cardamom pods, cinnamon sticks and whole cloves —each about an ounce in weight—in a cookie-sheet or a pie shell. Preheat the oven at 200°. Bake the spices for about 30 minutes stirring them once or twice. At the end of this time, take out the spices. Shell the cardamom, discard their shells and gather the seeds. Mix the cardamom seeds, the cinnamon sticks and the cloves in a dry jar of an electric blender. Grind the spices together till they form a fine powder. This amount will make a few teaspoons of ground *masala* which can last for a long time. If stored in a tightly closed jar it will stay fresh for months.

RICE

Rice will be dealt with in greater detail in the chapter on rice, but I would like to make some comments here. Rice is a very important food source to a great number of people in the world. There are many varieties of rice and an almost limitless number of delicious preparations. In the West, rice is thought of as a substitute for potatoes. This I think is a gross underestimation of rice as a valuable food source. While it is true that most rice marketed here is the polished white variety which does have most of the food values removed; it does not mean that the other varieties of rice such as parboiled rice, natural rice, brown rice, converted rice or naturally hulled rice should be downgraded. Rice is more than just a starch and western food analysts have yet to discover the true and valuable nature of rice.

Ingredients

GHEE

Ghee is butter that has all the milk solids removed. In the West there is a preparation known as clarified butter which closely approximates *ghee* but is not as pure or buttery. Most recipes that call for *ghee* will also allow for the substitution of ordinary sweet butter to be used in the place of *ghee*. Well worth the effort, *ghee* is fairly simple to prepare. Take one or more sticks of sweet butter and place in a low shallow pot over the lowest flame possible. It is important that the butter be not allowed to burn; it should only bubble until the milk solids appear as a froth of small particles floating on the top. This process should be repeated, each time removing as much of the froth as possible. After this removal of solids has been completed there should be left a clear, slightly yellow liquid looking somewhat like oil. Turn off the flame and let the *ghee* cool for 5 minutes. Now strain the liquid through a piece of muslin cloth and store in a jar. *Ghee* can be stored for quite a long time because it is the milk solids that turn rancid in butter, not the butterfat. In India where there are no refrigerators people store large amounts of *ghee* in cans in some cool spot. This is advisable only if the *ghee* is absolutely pure. When *ghee* is refrigerated it turns into a solid that can be brought back to a liquid by heating over a low flame. *Ghee* is most popularly used as a spread over freshly made Indian breads such as *chapatis* and *parothas*.

DALS (LENTILS OR SPLIT PEAS)

Dal, which literally means split peas, is an important component to most Indian meals. *Dals* contribute a significant amount of protein to the vegetarian diet. Most of the Indian *dals* such as *mung dal, toor dal, urad dal* and *masoor dal* are available through health and spice stores or through the mail-order addresses listed. The yellow and green split peas sold in local markets make very good *dal*. These lentils, as they are known, can keep their freshness for a number of months.

NUTS

Nuts such as cashews, peanuts, almonds and pistachios are often-used ingredients in Indian cooking. Aside from their high protein value nuts give a crunchy texture to a number of dishes.

VEGETABLE OIL

You may use any vegetable oil such as safflower oil, corn oil, sesame seed oil or peanut oil to cook Indian dishes, although many Indians cook with peanut oil. I prefer peanut oil because of the distinctive flavor that it gives to food. In certain parts of India people use coconut oil and mustard seed oil which also imparts a distinctive flavor to their regional dishes. The less refined the oil is the greater the food value will be. Oil that is used for sautéing vegetables cannot be reused, but oil that is used for deep frying can be used twice. Olive oil should not be used because of its heaviness and strong flavor.

Ingredients

WHOLE WHEAT PASTRY FLOUR

If you can obtain this consistency of flour, it is preferred to either all-purpose white flour or regular, ground, whole wheat flour for the preparation of Indian breads. All-purpose flour will not make the type of dough that is required for *puris* and *chapatis*. If whole wheat pastry flour is unavailable to you, then you can mix equal amounts of regular whole wheat flour and unbleached all-purpose flour together. This mixture of flours is adequate for making Indian breads.

KITCHEN EQUIPMENT

Your kitchen probably has all the utensils listed except perhaps for the wok or *kadhai*.

PATLI (ROLLING BOARD)

In India rolling boards are round to facilitate the rolling of round Indian breads such as *chapatis*.

JARA (SLOTTED METAL SPOON)

This spoon is used for draining off excess oil while deep frying. The Japanese style of draining spoon made out of wire mesh is excellent for this purpose.

VELAN (ROLLING PIN)

Indian rolling pins are solid pieces of wood, wider in the middle and gradually tapering off to the ends. It has been my experience that this shape is the best for rolling a near perfect round dough necessary for a number of different Indian breads, although any rolling pin or even a bottle will work.

KADHAI OR WOK

Kadhai is the Indian name and wok the Japanese name for this important cooking utensil. Because of this utensil's shape it is used both for deep frying and for sautéing vegetables. When cooking in a *kadhai* you use less oil to cook with than with a conventionally shaped pot. Also with a wok the oil used for deep frying lasts longer because there is less tendency for the oil to burn off. If you do not have a wok, you can use any shallow pot for deep frying.

HEAVY IRON PAN

For roasting Indian breads such as *chapatis* always use the heavy iron pans. Also for sautéing certain leafy vegetables such as cabbage an iron pan is perfect.

Beverages

The two most important drinks in India are water and tea, in that order. Water is taken many times during the day in India's hot climate. To most people of the world water serves as the primary thirst quencher, all other drinks being luxuries.

Very close to an Indian's heart is his or her cup of tea. Tea is usually introduced to children in India when they are still infants. Tea is prepared for every meal and very little reason is necessary to make a pot of tea at other times during the day. Because tea acts as a stimulant it has played an important role as a social tonic in most of Asia's recorded history. The act of serving tea to show one's hospitality is an age-old custom in most of the East. Very important tea ceremonies, each with a unique way of serving and preparing the golden aromatic liquor, have existed and have been carried down through time for thousands of years.

There is a well-known story in Chinese mythology which accounts for the origin of tea. A Buddhist monk, despite his best efforts, could not keep from dozing off when he tried to concentrate on his meditation. This caused him so much grief that he finally cut off his eyelashes to punish himself. At the very spot where the eyelashes landed on the ground there began to grow a tea plant. The monk took the plant and brewed it, using the beverage to refresh himself and to keep him awake while meditating. It seems that tea did actually originate in China, for even to this day many parts of the world including India, the Soviet Union and parts of Africa use the word *chai* as their word for tea.

Aside from its value as a stimulant, tea is also known to have a great deal of healing and soothing properties. It seems that tea has been prescribed for relief from colds and sore throats since the beginning of civilization. Much can be said for the soothing potential of tea. Indians are very much in love with the comforting warmth that a cup of good tea radiates through the body. Almost wherever you go in India you are greeted with a cup of tea. If you go to a store to purchase a costly item such as a silk sari and you seem to be a promising customer, the merchant will serve you endless cups of delicious *garam masala chai* (hot spicy tea), cooked with rich, thick buffalo milk. Even a person's relationship to another person may dictate the way tea is prepared. In the State of Gujarat, where I grew up, there is an old maxim which states that if you are preparing some tea and a respected friend enters the house you add extra milk to make up the needed cup. If a person enters of questionable importance, however, you just add enough water to make the extra cup.

The use of the word tea has been generalized in the West to include beverages made from other plants that are actually much different from the tea plant. There is *only one* species of plant that qualifies as a tea plant. There are, however, different varieties of tea that yield distinct flavors due, in part, to the locations of the tea plantations. Basically tea leaves are either the black fermented type or the green unfermented variety. These two types refer to the treatment the leaves receive after they are picked. Most Indian tea is of the black fermented type, although some green tea is pro-

Beverages

duced and drunk in parts of Northern India. Most green teas today come from China, Japan and Southeast Asia. At one time Chinese tea was the only tea people in the western world drank, but gradually the more flavorful and aromatic teas of India and Ceylon started to increase in popularity until today they are the most widely consumed of the two.

Traditionally green teas are brewed in water and served with or without sugar, but with no milk. Black teas, on the other hand, are brewed in water, or a combination of milk and water and, in India, served already sweetened. Here are some of the ways that tea is prepared in India.

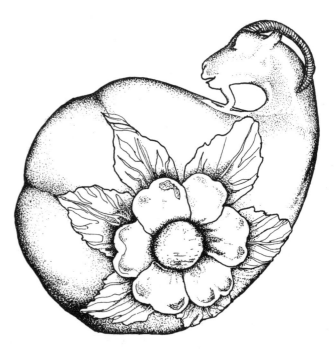

CHAI

2 cups water
1 cup milk
1 teaspoon loose black tea
sugar or honey to taste

The quantities indicated will yield 3 cups of tea and the same proportions for milk and water should be carried out when preparing greater or lesser amounts. The only variable is the strength of the tea. Such teas as Darjeeling, Ceylon and Assam are very strong and only a heaping teaspoon is necessary to prepare 3 cups of tea. Other loose black teas such as Orange Pekoe or a mixture may require 2 or even 3 teaspoons of tea for the same amount of milk and water. Heat the milk and water in a pot or saucepan over a moderate flame. The critical time in brewing tea is the point at which the water and milk begin to boil. Be waiting for the milk and water mixture to boil, for if left unattended it will boil over the sides of the pot. Allow the mixture to froth up as it begins to boil and then remove from the heat. Immediately add the loose tea and cover tightly. Let the tea seep for a few minutes stirring it once. The tea is ready when it is somewhat orange in color. In India tea is served already sweetened as it is assumed that everyone loves very sweet tea. I think it is better to prepare the tea without sugar and let the drinker add whatever amount of honey or sugar he prefers. It is good to buy tea in large amounts so that you can get used to the strength and brewing characteristics of that particular tea. You will get to know that a certain tea brews to perfection in five minutes yet another tea takes seven. This is important for if the tea leaves are left in the pot too long the tea will taste bitter. Always strain the tea leaves out of the tea when you feel it has become completely brewed.

Beverages

MASALA CHAI

2 cups water
1 cup milk
1 teaspoon loose black tea
3 pinches ground garam masala or
    1 whole cardamom and
    2 whole cloves and
    1 small stick cinnamon

Prepare in the same manner as regular *chai* explained in the previous recipe. When it comes time to add the tea, also add the ground *garam masala* (hot spices) or the fresh cardamom, cloves and cinnamon. The whole spices should be removed when straining the tea. *Masala chai* can be very effective in relieving the symptoms of a cold.

ENGLISH TEA

1 teapot freshly boiled water
1 cup milk
sugar or honey
1 or more teaspoons loose black tea

I have heard many people say that they thought the British had introduced the beverage of tea and milk to India and to the rest of the world. This is quite far from the truth as it was the Chinese who brought tea to India. Only in modern times have the British acquired the habit of drinking tea and milk, after learning of it from India. When the British were in India as colonialists, they segregated the tea water, the milk and the sugar. This became known as "English tea" or "tray tea." To the poor but practical Indian it seemed like an extravagance to have a separate teapot, milk server and sugar bowl plus utensils every time tea was served.

Place one or more teaspoons of tea at the bottom of a teapot, depending on the strength of the tea and the number of cups desired. Pour freshly boiled water over the tea and cover the teapot. If the teapot does not have a built-in strainer, then a separate strainer should be served with the tea. The tea should be allowed to brew for a few minutes. In a separate saucepan the milk should be heated until it boils and then it is transferred to a milk server. Serve the brewed tea still in the teapot and let the guests take their own milk and sugar.

ICED TEA

6 cups water
3 teaspoons loose black tea
3 or 4 mint leaves (optional)
3 fresh lemons
sugar

This beverage is becoming somewhat popular in the larger cities of India and is a big favorite in the West. On a hot day iced tea is especially refreshing and is quite good at quenching great thirst.

Boil 3 cups of water. If you like mint iced tea, add the mint along with the black tea to the boiled water and cover; remove from heat and let stand for a few minutes. Strain the brewed tea into a serving pitcher and add 3 glasses of ice-cold water, the juice of 3 lemons and sugar to taste. Mix this well and pour into individual glasses into which ice cubes have been placed. This will make 8 to 10 glasses of iced tea.

KASHMIRI CHAI

3 cups water
1 teaspoon green tea
1/4 teaspoon freshly chopped ginger

The only Indian people that I know of who drink green tea live in Kashmir and Dehra Dun. In the rest of India green tea is used as a remedy for colds and indigestion.

Pour the boiled water over the loose green tea. Add the finely chopped pieces of ginger and cover. Allow the tea to brew for a few minutes and serve with honey. When used to cure indigestion this remedy brings very quick and soothing relief.

SOUTH INDIAN COFFEE

One of my biggest surprises in traveling through India was being told in restaurant after restaurant in Tamil Nadu, that the only drink being served was coffee, that tea was not even available. Who would ever think that tea would not be readily available in any place in India? Although I had never acquired the taste for coffee in America, I enjoyed the thick rich milk coffee prepared throughout South India. The coffee there is primarily a mixture of hot milk and coffee, similar to café au lait. The difference is that the coffee is mixed back and forth between two cups until it has acquired a thick creamy consistency, almost like the Italian cappucino made with an espresso machine.

Beverages

BEVERAGES MADE FROM MILK AND BUTTERMILK

Milk and buttermilk drinks are most popular in India where they are valued for their taste as well as their high nutritional value. A poor person in India, who could not afford the luxuries of milk and butter, would drink the relatively inexpensive skimmed buttermilk, which is the by-product of certain dairy products such as butter and yogurt. This skimmed buttermilk has most of the butterfat removed and is similar to the skimmed milk sold here that is popular with calorie-conscious people. Highly prized in India is buffalo milk which is very sweet and creamy. Goat milk is the least popular milk as it has a tendency to smell like the goat it came from. Here are some popular *doodh* drinks, as milk is called in Hindi, that will reward you with good health and fine flavor.

KESAR DOODH (SAFFRON MILK)

1 glass milk
1 cardamom pod
1 whole clove
1 small stick cinnamon
4 to 5 threads saffron
2 tablespoons chopped almonds or cashews
honey

On the eleventh day of each month devout Hindus will eat only fruits, nuts, milk and honey. This day is called *Ekadeshi*, and *kesar doodh* is a favorite drink for those who can afford this rich delicacy.

Soak the strands of saffron in 3 tablespoons of warm milk for about 10 minutes. In a separate pot heat the milk, and when it is hot add the spices, the soaked saffron and the milk in which the saffron was soaked. Allow the milk mixture to stand for a few minutes, stirring occasionally. The milk should turn slightly yellow from the saffron. Stir again and strain out the whole spices. Add the chopped nuts and honey to taste. This drink is especially good when taken just before bedtime.

LASSI (BUTTERMILK DRINK)

3 cups buttermilk or yogurt
1 cup water
pinch salt
pinch cumin powder
ice cubes

The buttermilk that is sold in America is much thicker than the buttermilk in India. I usually add equal amounts of water and buttermilk together to get the consistency of buttermilk that is drunk in India. Buttermilk can also be made from plain yogurt by combining equal amounts of water and yogurt and stirring well.

Lassi is the milkshake of India. It is thicker than regular buttermilk drunk with the meal. It is a very popular drink throughout much of India. There are three ways of serving *lassi*—sweet, salted or plain.

For making plain or salted *lassi,* break some ice cubes into small pieces and fill a tall glass about a quarter of the way with the crushed ice pieces. Now mix together the buttermilk and water or yogurt and water and beat to a smooth consistency with a fork, blender or electric mixer. Add this mixture to the glass of chopped ice. Add the cumin and for a salted *lassi,* the salt. Mix together well and serve either with food or as a drink by itself.

MITHI LASSI (SWEET LASSI)

1 cup buttermilk or yogurt
1 cup water
2 tablespoons sugar
few drops rose water
ice cubes, crushed

Beat the buttermilk or yogurt together with the water using a fork or electric mixer until it has a smooth consistency. Pour into a tall glass with crushed ice. Add the sugar and rose water, stir and serve.

GARAM MASALA DOODH (HOT FLAVORED MILK)

1 glass milk
1 cardamom pod
1 whole clove
1 small stick cinnamon
honey or sugar to taste

Heat the milk in a saucepan but do not boil. Add the whole, uncrushed pod of cardamom, the whole clove and the piece of cinnamon. Cover the milk and let stand over a low heat for a few minutes. Remove from the heat, stir well and strain out the whole spices. The amount of honey or sugar which is added is not fixed and is left to individual taste. Serve in a cup or glass. This drink is excellent on cold days.

Beverages

MANGO JUICE

10 or 12 small juice mangos
brown sugar
pinch nutmeg or dried ginger

Most fruit juices available in the West, such as orange juice and apple juice go very well with Indian food and supply a great deal of vitamin C. In India there is only one fruit abundant enough for the people to make juice from and this is the mango. The type of mango used for juice is small, about the size of a clenched fist, and soft to the touch. Unfortunately mangos are very expensive in many parts of North America. If you are lucky enough, however, to run across some very ripe, small mangos at a reduced price, this drink is well worth the effort and expense.

Wash the mangos with water. Gently roll the unskinned mango between your palms until it becomes quite soft to the touch. Now cut off the tip of the mango where it comes to a point. With a firm, steady pressure squeeze the juice from the mangos into a large bowl. More juice can be extracted from the peel and pit after the squeezing of the whole mango yields no more juice. After all the liquid has been extracted, strain the juice through a fine strainer to remove any mango pulp. Add a pinch of nutmeg or dried ginger and some brown sugar, depending on how sweet the mangos are. Serve at room temperature or chilled and enjoy.

SUGARCANE JUICE

I include this beverage because it is such a wonderful drink and because I miss it so much. Fresh sugarcane is difficult enough to secure in most areas, but even more difficult to obtain would be the wringer-type apparatus that is used by street vendors who sell sugarcane juice all over India. A sugarcane is a six-foot length of bamboo-like stalk. A small piece of sugarcane is the Indian child's candy bar, full of sweet juice yet not harmful to the teeth. A common sight in the cities of India is the sugarcane-juice vendor pushing these long poles of sugarcane through his hand-operated juice extractor that appears to be very similar to the old-style hand clothes wringers. At one end of the machine there is a pot which collects the juice. Usually right below are the eager hands of young children clutching small coins with hopes that the next glass will be theirs. The vendor adds some lemon juice and a pinch of ginger, along with a big piece of ice, to make a cooling and satisfying drink, better than any cola drink imaginable. If you could taste sugarcane juice only once, you would understand my enthusiasm. If you happen to be walking down a street in Bombay on a hot day and come across a sugarcane-juice vendor, ask him for *ek ganna-ka-ras* (one sugarcane juice). You will be glad you did.

ANISE DRINK

2 tablespoons anise seeds
2 tablespoons sugar
juice of 1/2 lemon
ice cubes
water

Anise seeds look like caraway seeds and smell like licorice. The taste of this drink is somewhat like root beer without the carbonation. First boil the anise seeds in 2 cups of water for 5 minutes. Then cover the pot, remove from heat and let the anise seeds brew for another 5 minutes. Pour this liquid, together with the seeds, into an electric blender and blend until all the seeds appear crushed. If a blender is not available, then the seeds must be ground in a mortar or crushed with a stone, as is done in India, before they are boiled. Now strain the liquid through a fine mesh strainer and add 2 cups of cold water. Mix in the lemon juice and sugar, stir until all the sugar is dissolved. Pour into glasses filled with ice cubes, stir again and serve. This should make 2 or 3 glasses depending on how much ice is put in each glass.

TAMARIND DRINK

12 fresh tamarind pods*
or a handful of dried tamarind
sugar
water

*see glossary

Various delicacies can be made from the tamarind fruit, a sweet-and-sour treat from the tropics that is common to many parts of the world. I have found fresh tamarind at grocery stores in Spanish-speaking areas where it is called *tamarindo*. It is also available through some mail-order, health-food and spice stores. If the dried tamarind is used, it must be first soaked in warm water for 15 minutes.

Remove the hard outer shell from the tamarind fruit and separate the pits from the pulp. Soak the pulp in a bowl filled with 4 cups of water, so that the tamarind softens. Next, pour the tamarind and water into an electric blender and mix well. The Indian way is to squeeze the presoaked tamarind by hand, slowly extracting its flavor by repeated soaking and squeezing. After blending, strain the liquid through a fine strainer to remove the pulp. Add enough sugar and water to counterbalance the sourness. Chill before serving.

Beverages

GINGER DRINK

2-inch length of fresh ginger root
juice of 1 lemon
brown sugar or honey
water

This beverage is prepared by people in India, Ceylon and parts of Indonesia. Fresh ginger has a very strong taste; therefore one 2-inch piece of ginger root is sufficient to make 6 glasses of beverage.

Peel the ginger and chop into fine pieces. You may use a cheese grater for this purpose. Boil the chopped ginger in 6 cups of water for 15 minutes. Strain out the ginger and add brown sugar or honey until sweet. Start with 1 teaspoon of sugar or honey for each glass and add more if the drink tastes too strongly of ginger. If the taste is still too strong, then dilute with hot water. Add the fresh lemon and serve hot or cold.

BHANG

Bhang is a liquid preparation made from the leaves of a hemp plant known as marijuana. *Bhang* is drunk on religious holidays such as *Shiv-Ratri,* the birthday of Lord Shiva in the Hindu religion. Shiva is well known for his quick temper, for when he becomes irritated, he is capable of destroying the entire world with his third eye. Therefore on Shiva's birthday, *bhang* is offered to him by his devotees and then it is taken by the people as a *prasadi* (that which is left over from God). In the city of Benares, which is considered to be the holiest place in the world by the 500 million Hindus, *bhang* is prepared everyday in many of the temples and is sold in stores and government shops.

Its use to enhance the religious experience among holy people has been practiced for thousands of years. Therefore, despite the state-wide prohibition by the Indian government, *bhang* is served freely in many holy communities throughout India. Many different preparations of *bhang* can be seen offered to the people in Benares. Here is one preparation I know of.

BHANG

2 cups water
1 ounce marijuana (fresh leaves and flowers
    of a female plant preferred)
4 cups warm milk
2 tablespoons blanched and chopped almonds
1/8 teaspoon garam masala*
1/4 teaspoon powdered ginger
1/2 to 1 teaspoon rosewater
1 cup sugar

*see glossary

Bring the water to a rapid boil and pour into a clean teapot. Remove any seeds or twigs from the marijuana, add it to the teapot and cover. Let this mixture brew for about 7 minutes. Now strain the water and marijuana through a piece of muslin cloth, collect the water that is strained and save. Take the leaves and flowers that remain in the piece of cloth and squeeze between your hands to extract any of the liquid that remains. Add this extracted liquid to the water that was left after straining. Now using a mortar and pestle, place the lump of leaves in the mortar and add about 2 teaspoons of warm milk. Slowly but firmly grind the milk and leaves together with the pestle (in India a grinding stone is used). Gather up the marijuana and squeeze out as much liquid as you can by pressing the lump between the palms of your hands. Repeat this process of adding milk, grinding together and extracting the liquid until you have used up about 1/2 cup of the milk. This process of grinding and extracting should be repeated about 4 to 5 times in all. Collect all the liquid that has been extracted and place in a bowl. By this time the marijuana will have turned into a pulpy mass. Now add the blanched and finely chopped almonds to the mortar (a few at a time) along with the marijuana pulp and some more warm milk. Grind the almonds, milk and pulp together until a fine paste is formed. Gather this paste together in your hands and squeeze out as much of the liquid as you can into a bowl and add to one of the other bowls of previously collected liquid. Repeat this process a few more times until all that is left are some fibers and nut meal. Discard the fibrous residue and combine all the liquid that has been extracted and collected into a single bowl, including the water that the marijuana was originally brewed in. Add to this liquid the *garam masala,* dried ginger and rose water. Add the sugar and any of the remaining milk. Chill the *bhang,* serve and enjoy.

Snacks and Chutneys

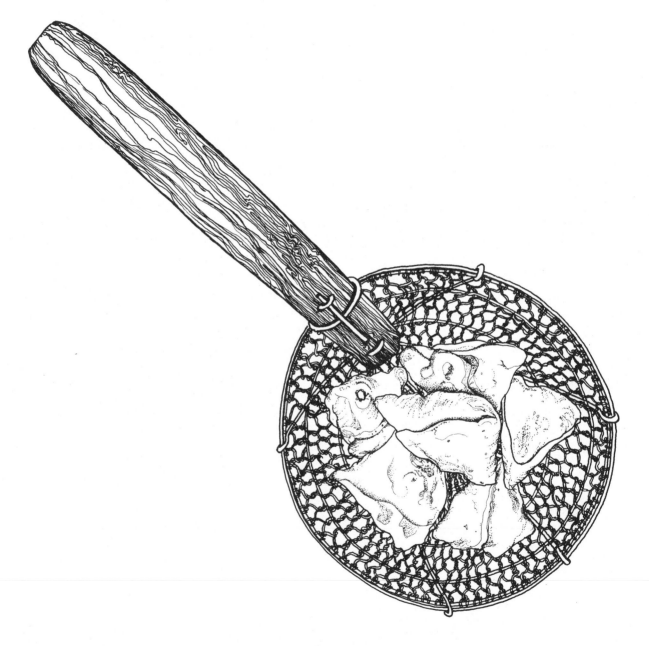

In cities and large towns, in railroad stations and bazaars throughout India, one is constantly tempted by the many small shops that offer tasty delicacies and tantalizing snacks, each served with a unique condiment known as chutney. The urban Indian may choose to pass up his usual lunch and instead substitute one or two of the many snacks which are available. Or if there is a wait between trains, as there often is, what better time to sample one of the many heat-rendering hot chutneys together with one of South India's delectable treats? These snacks, known as *farasan*, are as popular throughout India as Italian pizza is in the United States, and as available. But in the innumerable villages and small towns where the great majority of India's population lives, there are no restaurants, no snack shops, no echoing hawkers cooking up penny treats. Instead you will find in each earthen-floored kitchen, women preparing the same snacks for their husbands and children each in her own particular fashion. These many snacks and chutneys are being prepared for lunches, or for appetizers for an important meal or as a special holiday treat. A good cook is known for her chutneys and snacks that she offers to her guests and family in addition to a multicourse meal. Even though good-tasting food is taken for granted in India, a snack or a chutney is something special to be admired and savored. Some of the snacks that I will describe are quick and easy to make while others require a greater degree of preparation and skill. Each will be rewarded by quickly emptied plates and a steady stream of accolades for the cook.

Snacks

PAKORA or BHAJIA
(DEEP FRIED VEGETABLES IN BATTER)
2 cups besan (chick-pea flour)*
1 cup water
1/2 teaspoon coriander powder
1/2 teaspoon cumin powder
1/8 teaspoon garlic powder (or 1 clove crushed)
1/4 teaspoon turmeric powder
1/4 teaspoon cayenne
1-1/2 teaspoons salt
pinch of baking soda
1 fresh lemon

Fresh vegetables that can be used:
1 small eggplant
1 potato, peeled
1 carrot, scraped
1 small onion
1 banana
1 celery stalk, leaves removed
(any of the vegetables may be ommited
   or others substituted)
2 cups peanut oil

*see glossary

In some parts of India this snack is called *pakora* while in other regions it is known as *bhajia* (ba-gea). Almost any vegetable can be used, including cauliflower buds, broccoli pieces or even such non-Indian ones as mushrooms or asparagus. Basically *bhajias* are diced vegetables coated with *besan* (chick-pea flour) batter and then deep fried in oil. In this manner they are similar to the Japanese preparation of *tempura;* the difference being that the batter for *tempura* is made from whole wheat flour while the *bhajia* batter is made from chick-pea flour.

To prepare the batter place chick-pea flour in a large mixing bowl. Gradually add the water, mixing it with the flour by hand. Make sure that you break up all the lumps of flour and add a little extra water if necessary to form a batter that has a consistency a little thicker than pancake batter. Next, add all the spices including the salt and the baking soda, mixing them well into the batter. Squeeze the lemon juice into the batter and mix again. Taste, correct the seasoning if necessary, cover and put aside.

The vegetables should be diced or thinly sliced. Those that take a long time to cook, such as potatoes and carrots, should be cut into smaller pieces than the rapid-cooking vegetables such as bananas or zucchini. Cut all the vegetables to be used before you begin to heat the oil. Pour the peanut oil into a wok or a shallow saucepan, if a wok is not available. Place the oil over a moderate flame until a small drop of batter, when placed in the oil, bubbles and rises to the surface. Place a handful of the diced vegetables into the batter and mix until each piece is completely covered with batter. Remove the coated vegetables, one at a time, from the batter and gently lower into the hot oil, being careful of any hot oil spatter. About 5 or 6 *bhajias* can be cooked at one time without overcrowding the wok. Deep fry the *bhajias* until they turn a reddish brown. Remove from the oil with a slotted spoon allowing the excess oil to drain back into the heated oil. Before serving place the *bhajias* between layers of paper towels to further remove any oil residue. Serve the *bhajias* hot as an appetizer, side dish or by themselves as a snack. *Bhajias* go well with any type of chutney, *raita* or plain yogurt.

If there is some leftover batter, it can be saved for a day or two when covered and refrigerated. If this is the case, a few tablespoons of water may be added to the batter before reusing to restore any of the water that might have evaporated.

Snacks

CHEESE PAKORA

1 cup cubed cheese (or panir)
2 cups besan (chick-pea flour)*
3/4 cups water
1/2 teaspoon each coriander powder, cumin
    powder, turmeric powder and cayenne
1/8 teaspoon garlic powder
1-1/2 teaspoons salt
1 fresh lemon
pinch baking soda
2 cups peanut oil

*see glossary

The variety of cheeses available in the West is almost totally unknown in India. The cheese that would be used for this recipe in India is called *panir. Panir* is a homemade cheese and the preparation will be described in the chapter on dairy products. I have been successful using hard cheeses such as cheddar or swiss to make delicious cheese *pakoras.*

First cut the cheese into cubes about the size of sugar cubes and set aside. Next, make the batter as in the previous recipe for *bhajia,* except that you use less water so that the batter will be thicker.

Now heat the oil in a wok or shallow saucepan and test its hotness by dropping a bit of batter into the oil. Again, the oil is ready when the bit of batter bubbles and rises to the surface immediately after being dropped in. When ready, take a few cubes of cheese and thoroughly cover them with batter until there is no cheese showing through anywhere. If it is not covered completely with a thick coat of batter there is a tendency for the melted cheese to ooze out into the oil. Gently slip the cubes into the hot oil and cook until they turn a golden brown. Remove the *pakoras* with a slotted spoon allowing the excess oil to drain off. Drain on paper towels and serve with yogurt or a *raita.*

GHIYA BHAJIA
2 cups grated ghiya (doodhi or opo)*
2 cups besan (chick-pea flour)*
2 cups vegetable oil for deep frying
2 teaspoons salt
few pinches baking soda
1/2 teaspoon coriander powder
1/2 teaspoon cumin powder
1/2 teaspoon turmeric powder
1/8 teaspoon garlic powder (or 1 clove crushed)
1/2 teaspoon cayenne
1 fresh lemon

*see glossary

In chapter five I will go into greater detail about Indian vegetables that are available in this country. Briefly, *ghiya* is shaped like a long smooth-skinned cucumber; it is light green on the outside and milk white on the inside. In California it goes by its Philippine name, *opo*. I have also seen it sold in Chinese neighborhood grocery stores. If you are lucky enough to come across this vegetable, here is a delightful snack that can be prepared from half the vegetable while the other half can be saved or used as a main-dish vegetable.

Remove the skin from one half of a 2-pound *ghiya* and refrigerate the unused portion. Finely shred the *ghiya* using the small holes of a grater, until you have collected 2 cups of the vegetable. Scoop up the shredded *ghiya* into the palms of your hands and squeeze out the excess water. In a mixing bowl add the *besan* to the shredded *ghiya* and mix with your hands until you have a very thick batter. If the *ghiya* still contains a lot of water and the batter appears too thin, then you can add a little more flour until the right consistency is reached. Add the rest of the ingredients and stir the batter well.

Heat the oil for deep frying and test for hotness. Using your hand gather up about a teaspoon of batter, form into a lumpy ball and gently ease into the hot oil. Five or six of these *bhajias* can be deep fried at one time. When reddish brown remove from oil and drain, using paper towels. Serve these *bhajias* with yogurt or with the yogurt soup described on page 62.

Snacks

VADA

1 cup urad dal, skinned*
1/8 teaspoon cayenne
or 1 small hot green chili pepper
1/2 teaspoon finely chopped fresh ginger
1/4 teaspoon cumin powder
pinch baking soda
1/2 fresh lemon
salt to taste
1-1/2 cups vegetable oil for deep frying

*see glossary

This dish is very simple to make, however it requires a little planning. Soak the *urad dal* for at least 6 hours in 2 cups of water. I usually decide to make this dish the day before so I can let the *dal* soak overnight. Wash the *dal* in running water until the water stays clear. Now strain the water out and using an electric blender turn the *dal* into a thick purée. This is the tricky part, at least for me. In India the *dal* is ground using a heavy grinding stone. I usually divide the *dal* into 4 parts when using the blender to avoid gumming up the blade with the paste-like *urad dal* purée. Sometimes a teaspoon of water helps the blender to purée the *dal,* but try not to add too much water. Keep pushing down the batter while it is being blended so that the *dal* stays in contact with the chopping blades.

Using a rolling pin, grind all the spices together until a paste is formed. Add this paste together with the baking soda and lemon juice to the *urad dal* batter and mix well.

Heat the oil over a moderate heat either in a wok or heavy saucepot. Gather up teaspoonful lumps of batter and deep fry in the oil. Fry the lumps of batter until they turn dark brown, remove from the oil, drain and serve hot with yogurt or *raita.* In India *vadas* are usually shaped like a doughnut with a hole in the middle. But to make them this way takes a lot of practice and they don't taste any different from the easily formed round version.

Snacks

DAHI-VADA

vadas (see previous recipe)
1 cup plain yogurt
1/4 teaspoon black mustard seeds
1 hot, dried, whole chili pepper
1 teaspoon butter

This popular dish is a favorite in India and is as much a dessert as a snack. For those who prefer not to eat deep-fried foods there is a step that removes practically any excess or accumulated oil after the *vadas* have been fried.

Prepare the vadas as in the previous recipe, but immediately after removing from the oil place in a bowl of cold water. Let the *vadas* soak in the water for at least 5 minutes. Gently remove the *vadas* from the water and without breaking them squeeze out all the water. This step removes any oil that is left and allows the vadas to soak up the yogurt mixture they will be served in. Place the squeezed-out *vadas* on a plate and put aside until the next step is complete.

Place the yogurt in a bowl and beat with a fork until smooth. In a frying pan heat the butter over a low heat. Add the mustard seeds and dried chili pepper (seeds removed) to the melted butter. In a few minutes the mustard seeds will begin to pop. When they stop crackling, add the butter mixture immediately to the well-beaten yogurt. Mix well, pour the yogurt over the already prepared *vadas* and chill. This is a very cooling snack on a hot day.

BATATA-VADA (POTATO-FILLED TREATS)

Batter

1 cup besan (chick-pea flour)*
1/4 cup water
1/4 cup yogurt
1 teaspoon lemon juice
1/4 teaspoon coriander powder
1/4 teaspoon cumin powder
1/8 teaspoon cayenne
1/2 teaspoon salt
few pinches baking soda
few pinches garlic powder

Filling

1/2 pound potatoes
2 tablespoons peanut oil
1/4 teaspoon black mustard seeds
pinch of hing (optional)*
1/8 teaspoon turmeric powder
1/2 teaspoon finely chopped fresh ginger
1/4 teaspoon salt
juice of 1/2 lemon
1-1/2 - 2 cups cooking oil

*see glossary

To make the filling, boil the potatoes until they are soft to the touch of a fork. Peel the skins and dice the boiled potatoes into small pieces. In a medium-size pot add the peanut oil and heat over a moderate flame; then add the mustard seeds. When the mustard seeds stop popping, add the optional pinch of hing and then immediately add the potatoes. Sauté the potatoes for 2 minutes and while still stirring the mixture add the turmeric and the rest of the spices. Sauté for another 5 minutes or until the potatoes lump together almost like mashed potatoes. Remove the pot from the heat squeeze in the lemon juice and let cool. After the potatoes have cooled down enough to be handled, mash them with your hands. When they are sufficiently mashed, mold them into firm round potato balls about the size of walnuts.

Now prepare the batter by first mixing the yogurt, water and lemon juice with a fork. Then add the *besan* and mix well to break all the lumps. Add all the other ingredients listed for the batter and mix again.

Pour cooking oil in a wok or pot and heat. The oil is hot enough when a piece of batter immediately bubbles to the surface. When the oil is ready, take a few of the potato balls and cover them with batter. Carefully put them into the hot oil trying not to upset the coating of batter. Fry the *batata-vadas* until they are golden brown. Drain on absorbent towels and serve alone or with either coriander or raisin chutney.

Snacks

SEV (NOODLES)
1 cup besan (chick-pea flour)*
1 tablespoon oil
2 tablespoons water
few pinches baking soda
1/2 teaspoon salt
1/8 teaspoon cayenne powder
1-1/2 cups oil for deep frying

*see glossary

This is an easy and quick snack to prepare. These noodles can be served with plain or fried rice or can be munched on during afternoon tea breaks.

In a large bowl measure out flour. Spread the tablespoon of oil over the flour and hand mix until all the flour feels wet. Now add the water, baking soda, salt and cayenne. Mix the dough up until it takes on the consistency of cookie dough. It might require a little kneading to get the dough stiff enough. Now heat the oil in a deep pot over a medium flame.

There are two methods of preparing the dough for noodles. The first involves rolling out individual noodles with the palm of your hands, and the second way involves a special utensil for forming the noodles. In the first method you should break off walnut-size chunks of dough and roll them out into one or more thin strips. This dough is easy to roll out and the noodle can be made as thin as you like. Drop these noodles into the hot oil until they turn almost red, remove with a slotted spoon and drain before serving. These noodles can be served either hot or cold and can be stored for a few days.

UPMA

2 tablespoons melted butter
1 teaspoon urad dal (optional)*
1/8 teaspoon black mustard seeds
1 medium onion, finely chopped
1 cup cream of wheat
2 cups water (hot but not boiling)
few pinches turmeric powder
salt and cayenne pepper to taste
1/2 teaspoon brown sugar or honey
1 tomato, cut up
1 lemon
2 tablespoons chopped mixed nuts (cashews,
    almonds, walnuts, peanuts)

*see glossary

Upma can be eaten for breakfast or used as a side dish substitute for rice or potatoes. As a meal in itself *upma* proves to be wholesome and nutritious. Very popular all over India, *upma* sometimes is made with a little *urad dal,* a unique flavoring, mostly used in Southern India.

If the *urad dal* is going to be used, it should be soaked in a few tablespoons of warm water for about half an hour. After it has been soaking it should be completely drained of water and set aside until needed.

Melt the butter in a large heavy frying pan over a low heat. Add the well drained *dal* (optional), mustard seeds and the chopped onion. When the onions turn brown and the mustard seeds stop popping, stir in the cream of wheat. Continually stir the mixture until a reddish color is apparent, then slowly start to add the hot water, stirring all the while so that the cream of wheat does not form lumps. Now add the turmeric, salt, pepper and sugar or honey. Stir until all the spices have been thoroughly mixed into the *upma.* Add the cut-up tomato, squeeze the lemon over the *upma* and stir again. Top this dish with chopped nuts and cover. Remove from the heat and let stand a few minutes before serving.

Snacks

SAMOSA

Filling

1 large or 2 small potatoes
1 carrot
1/2 cup fresh or canned shelled peas
1 tablespoon vegetable oil
1/4 teaspoon black mustard seeds
1/8 teaspoon ground garam masala*
1/8 teaspoon turmeric powder
1/8 teaspoon finely chopped fresh ginger
1/4 cup finely chopped onion or scallion
1/2 teaspoon salt

Dough

1 cup all-purpose flour
1 tablespoon melted and cooled butter or ghee*
1/2 teaspoon salt
2 tablespoons water
2 cups oil for deep frying

*see glossary

The filling should be prepared first so that it will be cool by the time the dough is finished. Peel the potato and carrot and dice into small pieces. In a medium-size pot heat about 3/4 of a cup of water. When the water becomes hot but does not boil, add the potatoes, carrot and peas. Tightly cover the pot and let the vegetables steam until they are fairly soft; this should take about 15 minutes. The heat should be moderate to low so that the water is not reduced too quickly. When the vegetables are soft but not mushy and all the water has been absorbed or cooked out, remove them to a mixing bowl. In another pot measure out the 1 tablespoon of oil and heat over a moderate flame. Add the mustard seeds and chopped onion or scallions. When the onions have browned, add the steamed vegetables and sauté for 5 minutes or until the potatoes are very soft. Add all the spices and salt while continuing to stir the mixture. When all the spices have been mixed in well, the filling is ready. Remove from the heat and allow to cool while you prepare the dough.

To make the dough for the half-moon-shaped shells first place the flour in a large mixing bowl. Rub into the flour the melted and cooled butter or *ghee,* making sure it is thoroughly worked into the flour. Add the salt and water and knead until a smooth dough is formed. If the dough appears very flaky, add a little water, a teaspoon at a time, and knead until the dough is a bit stiff. Now using the bottom part of your palms knead the dough using a pushing motion as you would to prepare clay. Continue to knead the dough until it feels even all over. The *samosa* jackets are now ready to be rolled out. If the dough is not to be used right away, it should be wrapped in a wet muslin cloth to keep it from drying out.

Break off a walnut-size piece of dough and flatten out using the palm of your hand. Sprinkle a little flour on a wooden board and with a rolling pin roll out the dough, trying to roll out round, thin shapes. The thin, circular jackets should be approximately 4 to 5 inches in diameter. Roll out as many circles as you want *samosas.* Take one rolled-out circle at a time and cut into two semi-circles of about equal size. Take one of the halves and moisten one side with a little oil. Now place about 2 tablespoons of the cooled vegetables in the center of the oiled half circle and gently spread around evenly but not quite to the edges of the dough. Take the other half circle and place on top of the vegetables. Using your fingers join the two pieces of dough so that the vegetables are completely enclosed. You should wind up with a half-circle *samosa* as pictured in the illustration. When all the *samosas* have been stuffed and sealed, they are ready for deep frying.

Heat the 2 cups of oil over a moderate flame. When sufficiently hot, place 2 or 3 *samosas* in the oil and cook for 5 minutes during which time they should have become brown. When they are brown, remove with a slotted spoon and allow the excess oil to drain back into the pot. Place on absorbent towels to remove any extra oil and serve hot with any chutney you like.

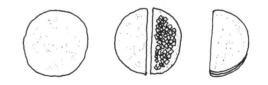

Snacks

DOSA (A LIGHT PANCAKE-LIKE SNACK)
1/2 cup urad dal*
1 cup rice
1 teaspoon salt
oil for greasing the skillet

*see glossary

Dosa is a thin, crisp, pancake-like snack that is served with a mildly hot sauce called *rasam*. *Dosa* is extremely popular all over South India. Almost a national snack, like pizza in America and crêpes in France, you will be able to find a *dosa* shop in even the smaller towns of South India. Any time is *dosa* time and it is not unusual for a *Madrasi* to enjoy a *dosa* for breakfast served with spicy *rasam*. Every South Indian housewife is knowledgeable in the ways of preparing *dosa*. Many hours are spent in the grinding and pulverizing of rice and *urad dal*, using heavy grinding stones in order to achieve the smooth paste necessary for a perfect *dosa*. The finer the paste, the thinner the *dosa* can be made. I have been reasonably successful using an electric blender, in place of the grinding stone, to prepare the paste batter. The preparation of *dosa* will take a little patience and some practice before you will be rewarded with perfectly formed *dosa*.

In two separate bowls soak the uncooked rice and the *urad dal*, using 2 cups of water for the rice and 1 cup of water for the *dal*. Let them soak a minimum of 6 hours or even better, overnight. When you are ready to begin, thoroughly wash and drain the rice and *dal*. Using an electric blender first grind the *dal* with 4 tablespoons of water. Try to make it as smooth as possible. Remove the puréed *dal* from the blender. Now grind the rice to a fine, smooth consistency using 1/2 cup of water. After you have ground both rice and *dal* to a smooth paste, mix them together with a fork. Add the salt and stir once again. Now let the *dosa* mix stand for 2 hours in a covered bowl.

After the 2 hours are up, grease a heavy skillet with 1/2 teaspoon oil and heat it over a high flame. Now stir up the batter and pour approximately 1/2 cup of the mixture into the center of the hot skillet. Immediately begin to spread the batter in a circular motion using the back of a wooden spoon. The art of making *dosa* lies in being able to make quickly a 9-inch diameter circle out of the batter before the heat of the skillet has begun to cook and harden the mixture. Try to spread the mixture as thinly and evenly as possible. The best *dosas* are those that come out almost paper thin, but this requires a certain amount of expertise. Cook the *dosa* about 7 minutes on each side or until golden brown. After the first side is cooked, loosen with a metal spatula and turn over. I've seen some cooks make *dosa* so thin that it was not necessary to cook on both sides. Many times the first *dosa* is not successful since the skillet needs to be "seasoned" by the first attempt. Add more oil to grease the skillet when it looks dry or the *dosas* are sticking too much. Cook all the *dosas* and serve hot with *rasam,* which is described in the next recipe.

RASAM

1/2 cup toor dal*
pinch baking soda (optional)
1 teaspoon salt
1/8 teaspoon turmeric powder
1 teaspoon shreds of coconut
1 tomato, diced
1 lemon or 2 pods fresh tamarind*
1 tablespoon vegetable oil
1/2 teaspoon black mustard seeds
1 dry red chili pepper cut in half
and seeded
or 1/8 teaspoon cayenne

*see glossary

Rasam is the thin sauce that is usually served with *dosa*, *idli* and other popular South Indian dishes. Its basis is *toor dal* which comes coated with an oil that acts as a preservative for the raw *dal*. Before using this *dal* it must be washed very thoroughly in hot water to remove the oily outer coating.

First boil 3 cups of water into which a teaspoon of salt has been added. Now wash the *toor dal* very well as indicated. Add the cleaned *dal* to the boiling water and cook covered for 20 minutes to 1/2 hour or until the *dal* is soft enough to be easily squashed between two fingers. If you add the pinch of soda it will help speed up the cooking of the *dal*. When the *dal* is soft, add 2 more cups water and mix well. Cook uncovered for another 15 minutes, by which time all the *dal* should be dissolved into a liquid. If there are still traces of undissolved *dal*, an egg beater or an electric blender could be used to complete the process. Stir the *dal* occasionally while it is cooking, and when completely dissolved add the turmeric, shreds of coconut, and a diced tomato. Squeeze in the lemon or add the tamarind pulp from the fresh pods after the shells and seeds have been removed. Cook another few minutes over a low heat, stir, remove from heat and keep covered.

In a separate small pot heat the tablespoon of oil over a medium flame. When hot add the mustard seeds and the halved and seeded chili pepper. When the mustard seeds begin popping and the chili becomes dark, add the entire contents of the pot to the *dal*. This should be accompanied by a sizzling sound and a smell that is characteristic of South Indian kitchens. If cayenne is used instead of whole dried chili, then only the mustard seeds should be cooked in the oil and the cayenne should be added to the *dal* after the oil and mustard seed mixture has been added. Stir and cover the *rasam* for a few minutes before serving with *dosa*.

Snacks

MASALA DOSA
(DOSA WITH A SPICY FILLING)
Dosa
see preceding recipe

Filling
1 pound potatoes
2 tablespoons vegetable oil
1 medium onion, finely chopped
1/4 teaspoon black mustard seeds
1/4 teaspoon turmeric powder
1 tablespoon chopped coriander leaves*
or 1/4 teaspoon coriander powder
1 fresh hot green chili, finely chopped
or 1/2 teaspoon cayenne
salt to taste
1/2 lemon

*see glossary

Before making the *dosa,* prepare the filling. First boil the potatoes in a big pot of water until they are soft but not mushy. Remove the cooked potatoes from the water, peel and cut into large cubes. In another pot heat the vegetable oil and add the chopped onion and mustard seeds. When the onions are browned, add the diced boiled potatoes, turmeric, salt, hot pepper and coriander. Sauté this mixture for 10 minutes until all the spices are well blended. Remove from the heat, squeeze the lemon juice over the filling, stir and cover until the *dosa* is ready.

Prepare the *dosa* as in *dosa* recipe. Place three tablespoons of filling in the center of each cooked *dosa.* Fold two ends of the *dosa* over the filling to form a sort of tube with the filling in the center. Serve hot with a separate bowl of *rasam.*

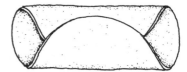

CHIVRA
(INDIAN STYLE MUNCHING STUFF)
1/2 cup chana dal*
2 tablespoons peanut oil
1 cup chopped mixed nuts (cashews,
  peanuts, almonds, etc.)
2 tablespoons ghee (clarified butter)*
3 cups pauva (puffed rice)*
or the same amount of puffed rice
  cereal (unsweetened)
pinch of hing*
1/2 teaspoon turmeric powder
1 teaspoon salt
2 tablespoons raisins
1 teaspoon sugar
1/4 teaspoon cayenne
1 lemon
1 tablespoon shredded coconut

*see glossary

This snack is popular during tea time or at any time. It can be stored in jars for future use and does not need refrigeration.

Soak the *chana dal* in 1 cup of water for an hour and drain. Use paper towels to pat the *dal* completely dry. Heat the 2 tablespoons of oil in a large frying pan or wok and add the dried *dal*. Sauté the *dal* until it appears red and crisp. Remove the cooked *dal* from the pan and set aside in a bowl. Add the chopped nuts to the same skillet or wok already greased from the *dal*. Sauté for a few minutes until all the nuts are glazed with a coating of oil. Remove the nuts and set aside. In a separate pot melt the butter or *ghee* over a low flame. When this is hot, add the *hing,* rice, salt and turmeric, and mix well. While sautéing these ingredients, continue to stir for 10 minutes and then turn off the heat. Add to this the already cooked *dal,* nuts, raisins, sugar and cayenne. Squeeze in the lemon and mix together thoroughly. Taste the *chivra* and correct the flavoring by adding more salt if necessary. Top the *chivra* with the coconut shreds and serve after it is cooled.

Chutneys

Chutneys

CHUTNEYS

In India a woman usually starts her day first by lighting the *sigri,* a portable cooking stove, and then preparing a fresh chutney for the day. Chutneys are similar in concept to western condiments such as mustard, relish and catsup. They are used as an added flavor and as an appetite stimulator to a meal. Chutneys are served in very small quantities and are not to be considered a side dish. They are usually very hot and spicy and therefore only the smallest amount, a teaspoon or less, is required to complement an Indian meal. Usually the chutney is placed at the edge of the plate or in an individual little dish. People who are not familiar with Indian food should be forewarned about the chutney before they sample it, lest they take too much. Chutneys are served with snacks, and no Indian meal can be considered complete without at least one chutney.

Two types of chutneys will be described in this section, the fresh chutneys that are made everyday for daily use and the more complex preserved chutneys. The preserved chutneys such as green mango, baby eggplant and lemon require many ingredients that are not available in the West, and also many of them require complicated procedures taking as much as two weeks to prepare. Fortunately these preserved chutneys are available already prepared and imported from India, in many stores carrying Indian foods and spices. If they are unavailable in your local area, they can be ordered from one of the spice houses listed at the end of the book. These preserved chutneys can keep for many months although they are expensive.

The preserved chutneys are also called pickles. Here are some recipes for pickles that are easily and quickly prepared.

Chutneys

GINGER PICKLES

1/2 pound fresh ginger root
2 tablespoons salt
2 tablespoons turmeric powder
4 to 6 lemons

Scrape the outside of the ginger roots as you would a carrot and cut into small pieces. Place the cut-up pieces of ginger in a bowl and mix in the salt, turmeric and the juice from 4 lemons. Put this mixture into a jar that can be tightly closed. Cut up 1 or 2 lemons into fine slices with the skin intact. Spread these lemon slices over the top of the ginger mixture in the jar and tightly close. Now leave this jar at room temperature for a week. At the end of this time the ginger pickles are ready to be served. The salt combines with the turmeric and lemon juice to produce a yellow liquid that turns the ginger into a sour, hot, salty pickle that is not so strong as raw ginger by itself. This pickle can be served with any meal. It should be stored in a refrigerator when not being used.

CARROT PICKLES

3 fresh carrots
2 teaspoons salt
1 teaspoon turmeric powder

This carrot pickle is quick and easy to make and can be eaten after 2 hours. Scrape carrots clean and cut into slender lengthwise strips. Place these carrot strips in a jar or bowl and sprinkle the salt and turmeric over them. Mix all ingredients. Let this stand at room temperature for 2 hours before eating. Refrigerate the unused carrot pickles. They will keep well for a few days.

HOT PEPPER PICKLES

12 hot green chilis
6 fresh lemons or limes, juiced
4 teaspoons salt
1 tablespoon turmeric powder

Cut the chilis in half lengthwise and remove the seeds and any pulp. Place in a bowl and add the lemon or lime juice, salt and turmeric. Mix and store in a tightly closed jar at room temperature for a week. At the end of the week these pickles are ready to be served, but be careful as they are very hot.

Chutneys

FRESH CHUTNEYS

Here are some chutneys that you can make fresh for everyday use. An electric blender is a great help in preparing many of these or, if you are so disposed, you can use the traditional stone-ground method. One word of caution when using an electric blender: allow the ingredients to settle down after they have been ground up before you remove the top of the blender. When grinding hot spices, the air inside the blender becomes filled with their hot essence and can be very irritating to your eyes and nose. So let things calm down inside the blender before you empty it. These chutneys are served in a dish, placed in the center of the dining area, and each person takes as much as he wishes.

PHODINO (MINT) CHUTNEY

1 cup chopped fresh mint leaves
1/2 cup chopped scallion with leaves
1 tablespoon finely chopped fresh ginger
2 fresh hot green chili peppers
1/2 teaspoon salt
1 lemon

Place the finely chopped mint, scallion, ginger and chili peppers in the blender together with the salt. Squeeze the lemon over the ingredients and blend the chutney to a fine paste. Let the air in the blender settle before removing the top. This is a fairly strong chutney, but extremely good. Serve with any of the dishes described in this book.

PEANUT CHUTNEY

1 cup shelled peanuts (roasted)
1/2 cup fresh coriander leaves*
or 1 teaspoon coriander powder
1 tablespoon finely chopped fresh ginger
2 fresh hot green peppers
or 1/2 teaspoon cayenne
1/2 cup plain yogurt
1 teaspoon sugar
1/2 teaspoon salt

*see glossary

Shell the peanuts and put aside. Finely chop the coriander, ginger and peppers. Place these ingredients in a blender along with the other spices, yogurt and shelled peanuts. Now blend until a fine but slightly coarse mixture is formed. If after awhile the ingredients do not blend into a uniformly fine mixture, then remove the chutney and let stand for an hour before reblending. During that hour the juices will soften any hard particles and allow the blender to turn the chutney into a smooth paste. This chutney can be served with any Indian meal and can be stored for a few days in a refrigerator.

Chutneys

564-5608

RAISIN CHUTNEY

1 cup raisins
1 tablespoon chopped fresh ginger
1/2 teaspoon cayenne
1/2 teaspoon salt
4 tablespoons water
1/2 lemon

This is another excellent tasting sweet-and-sour chutney that is easy to make. Put all the ingredients listed in a blender, adding the lemon juice last. Blend until all the ingredients form a coarse paste. Remove from the blender and serve with any snack or meal. This chutney will keep in a refrigerator for about two weeks.

CORIANDER CHUTNEY

1 cup finely chopped fresh coriander leaves*
1 tablespoon finely chopped fresh ginger
1 large or 2 small fresh hot green chilis
1 teaspoon brown sugar
1/2 teaspoon salt
1/2 lemon

*see glossary

Thoroughly wash the coriander leaves, and chop them finely. Cut the fresh green chili and the fresh ginger into fine pieces. Put the finely chopped coriander, chili pepper and ginger in a blender together with the brown sugar and salt. Squeeze the lemon over the ingredients, close the blender and mix until a paste is formed. Wait a minute or two until the air inside the blender settles down, then remove the chutney and serve with any Indian meal.

TAMARIND CHUTNEY

1/2 cup tamarind pulp, seeds removed*
1 tablespoon finely chopped fresh ginger
1 tablespoon brown sugar
3 tablespoons water
1/4 teaspoon cayenne

*see glossary

Method: soak in water to soften pulp.

Remove the hard outer shell and the seeds from the tamarind so that you are left with only the pulp. If you are using the preserved, already shelled tamarind it should be soaked in warm water for half an hour before using. Chop the ginger very finely and put into the blender along with all the other ingredients. Blend to a fine paste and it is ready to serve. This is one of my favorite chutneys because of its characteristic sweet-and-sour hotness. Tamarind chutney goes well with any Indian snack or meal and is especially good with *pakoras* and *samosas*.

Chutneys

GARLIC CHUTNEY

3-4 garlic cloves, very finely chopped
2 teaspoons cayenne
1/2 teaspoon coriander powder
1/2 teaspoon cumin powder

Unlike the previous recipes this is a "dry" chutney. It takes the appearance of a dry mound rather than a smooth purée as do the other chutneys. The proportions of the ingredients can vary according to the individual tastes of the cook. In South India, some coconut is usually added to garlic chutney.

Put the chopped garlic in the center of a wooden board and heap the other ingredients around and on top of the garlic. Using a rolling pin grind the ingredients together. When pressed by the rolling pin, the garlic will release a juice which forms a kind of dry paste with the other spices. Keep rolling until all the ingredients are well mixed together. Gather together the paste that sticks to the wooden board and the rolling pin and consolidate it into a single mound. Store in a dish and keep refrigerated. This chutney is added to some vegetables and *dals* while they are being cooked. Some people prefer to serve it with the meal as with the other fresh chutneys. If you do use it as a fresh chutney be careful as it is extremely hot!!

COCONUT CHUTNEY

1/2 fresh coconut (1 cup grated)
1/2 cup water
3 tablespoons tamarind pulp*
  or the juice of 1 lemon and
    and 1 tablespoon brown sugar
2 hot green chilis
  or 1/2 teaspoon cayenne
1 tablespoon chopped fresh ginger
1/2 teaspoon salt
1 cup fresh coriander leaves*
*see glossary

Grate the coconut meat into fine pieces. If the tamarind is to be used it should be soaked in water for 15 minutes prior to being used. Put the coconut, 1/2 cup water, tamarind pulp and coriander in a blender. Remove the seeds from the chili peppers, finely chop the peppers and add them with the chopped ginger to the blender. If the tamarind is not being used, then the mixture of lemon juice and brown sugar should be added to the other ingredients. Add the salt and blend to a smooth consistency. This chutney is most popular in the coastal areas of India where coconuts are grown.

Chutneys

DATE CHUTNEY

1 cup chopped and pitted dates
   (preferably dry kind)
1 tablespoon chopped fresh ginger
1/2 teaspoon cayenne
1/2 teaspoon salt
4 tablespoons water
2 tablespoons chopped fresh coriander leaves*
   (optional)
1 lemon
or 1/2 cup tamarind pulp,* seeds removed

*see glossary

Add all the ingredients, except the lemon juice, to the blender and mix until well blended. Remove the chutney from the blender and place in a bowl. Squeeze the lemon juice over the chutney and mix well with a fork. This is another fine chutney that goes well with almost any Indian food or snack.

RAITAS

A *raita* is a yogurt-based dish that is usually served to impart added flavor to a snack, salad or main dish, rather than as a dish by itself. Most *raitas* contain *rai* (mustard seeds) and are made with yogurt mixed with a fruit or vegetable. Here are some quick and easily prepared *raitas* that are perfect for all occasions. They require no cooking which is a special treat on hot days.

CUCUMBER RAITA

2 cups plain yogurt
1/8 teaspoon black mustard powder*
1/2 teaspoon salt
1 large cucumber, peeled and diced
few pinches cayenne
1 tablespoon fresh chopped coriander
   leaves* (optional)

*see glossary

Put the yogurt in a bowl and beat lightly with a fork until free flowing and smooth. Now add the mustard powder, salt and diced cucumber, and stir again until well mixed. Top the *raita* with a few pinches of cayenne and the chopped coriander leaves. If you wish, you can chill the *raita* before serving.

BANANA RAITA

2 cups plain yogurt   [Blend]
1 ripe banana
1/8 teaspoon black mustard powder*   [or dry mustard]
few pinches cayenne
1/4 teaspoon salt

*see glossary

Lightly beat the yogurt with a fork until it has a smooth, free-flowing consistency. Slice the banana into the yogurt. Add the salt, mustard powder and cayenne. Mix well before serving.

CARROT RAITA

1 large carrot
2 cups plain yogurt
1/4 teaspoon salt
1/8 teaspoon cumin powder
1/8 teaspoon cayenne
1 tablespoon chopped corainder leaves*
or chopped parsley leaves

*see glossary

Clean and scrape the carrot, grate with a cheese grater and put aside. Lightly beat the yogurt in a bowl until smooth. Add the salt, cumin, cayenne and grated carrot. Garnish the top of the *raita* with the chopped coriander or parsley and serve.

RADISH RAITA

1 cup grated radish
2 teaspoons salt
2 cups plain yogurt
1/8 teaspoon cumin powder
few pinches cayenne

Grate the radishes and place in a bowl. Add the salt to the grated radishes and using your hands, squeeze out any excess water. The squeezing also removes some of the salt and the hotness of the radishes. In a separate bowl beat the yogurt with a fork until smooth. Add the radishes and then the cumin to the yogurt and mix well. Top the *raita* with a few pinches of cayenne and serve.

CABBAGE RAITA

2 cups plain yogurt
1 cup very finely shredded green cabbage
salt and pepper to taste
1/8 teaspoon cumin powder

Lightly beat the yogurt with a fork until very smooth and free flowing. Add the remainder of the ingredients to the yogurt and mix well. Place in the refrigerator for an hour to chill. Stir just before serving. Some people like to steam the cabbage before mixing it with the yogurt.

CACHUMBER (INDIAN SALAD)

2 big tomatoes (about 1 pound)
6 scallions or 1 small onion
1 large cucumber
1/2 lemon
salt and black pepper

This is the Indian version of a salad. Wash the tomatoes and chop them into small cubes. Clean the scallions or the onion and chop into small pieces. Skin the cucumber and slice or dice into thin pieces. Mix all the ingredients. Now squeeze the lemon over and add salt and pepper to taste. Mix, chill and serve.

Serves Four

Milk and Dairy Products

One reason why the cow is sacred in India is the wondrous milk that she provides. The nutritional importance of milk cannot be overstated. To a vegetarian, milk is a prime source of proteins, calcium and vitamins. Milk is the only food on which a newborn infant will thrive. It is a miracle of nature that causes life-sustaining milk to flow from a mother's breast; it is no less a miracle of nature that enables the cow to supply mankind with this vital food. Milk contains almost all the necessary nutritional components to build and nourish a healthy body. So you see why the cow is revered in India.

Here in the West, milk and dairy products are almost taken for granted. In India, however, it is a great shame that many people cannot afford to drink a sufficient amount of milk necessary for proper growth and good health. Because of this, good health has become a luxury, reserved for those who can afford the price of milk. Often I have heard doctors tell India's poor people that they should drink more milk, without first considering how these people will be able to pay for this luxury. Hopefully modern technology will one day help make the cow's milk readily available to all people.

Although milk from the goat and the graceful buffalo is also available, the cow, by and large, is the greatest source of milk. Lord Krishna, as a young man, is frequently portrayed in temples throughout India in constant companionship with the gentle cows and milkmaids; or stealing butter from his mother's closet with the aid of his friends, the monkeys. I have heard India's buffalo referred to as water buffalo, probably to distinguish them from the native bison. But in India we know them only as buffalo and especially value them for the thick, rich, creamy milk that they provide. In fact, the part of India that I come from is known for its good cooking, its pretty women and its rich, sweet buffalo milk. It is a great honor to be served tea that has been prepared with the more expensive buffalo milk.

The least popular milk is goat's milk. Although goat's milk is given to children and is as nutritious as cow's milk, it is rarely taken by adults because of its characteristic goat-like flavor and smell. Even when mixed with strong tea and sugar it is easy for an Indian to recognize the taste of the goat milk. In India one would never serve a guest goat milk in any form. Mahatma Ghandi once took a vow not to drink milk. For a while this was fine, but when his health became poor his doctors stressed the need for milk. In order to remain partially faithful to his vow, he agreed only to drink goat's milk. This was a sure indicator to the people of India of Ghandi's great self-sacrifice and discipline.

Yogurt is an important and extremely popular dairy product throughout India. Yogurt will be served with lunch and dinner and many dishes are made with it. As a source of protein and calcium, yogurt is second only to milk. Yogurt's importance to an Indian meal will be discussed more fully later in this chapter.

The watery liquid that is left after most of the milk solids and butterfat have been removed in the process of making butter from yogurt is called *chhash*. This watery by-product is what many of

Milk

the poor people use as their "milk." *Chhash* is sold very inexpensively or given away free as there are no other uses for it.

Cheese processing is almost unknown in India, perhaps because there is no surplus of milk. In all India there are a handful of dairies that produce cheese, but the cost is so prohibitive that it is almost unknown to most of the people. The homemade soft cheese called *panir* is not eaten by itself but rather is used in cooking other dishes.

I have tried to cover the range of milk and dairy products that have been used by the people of India for centuries. Not only is milk an important dietary staple in India but it also carries with it a certain spiritual quality that probably stems from the people's awareness of milk's great value. Following are the recipes for homemade yogurt, buttermilk, *panir* and several dishes made from these dairy products.

BUTTERMILK

1 cup yogurt
1 cup water

Buttermilk is another popular and refreshing drink in India. When served as a beverage the buttermilk is of a much thinner consistency than the buttermilk that is commercially available in the West. In fact I usually dilute equal amounts of water and store-bought buttermilk to arrive at the consistency of buttermilk as it is served in India.

To make buttermilk from yogurt is a very simple process. Simply add one cup of water to one cup of yogurt and stir well with a fork or an egg beater or blend briefly in an electric blender. The finished product is buttermilk that can be served with meals or drunk by itself.

PANIR (CHEESE)
1 quart milk
juice of 1/2 lemon and 1/2 cup plain yogurt
or juice of 1 lemon

This is a recipe for a "raw" soft cheese called *panir*. *Panir* is not eaten by itself but is used in the preparation of certain sweets and dishes such as the one following for *matar panir*. What you will end up with at the end of this recipe is a soft, crumbly, cheese-like substance that will be an ingredient in other recipes in this book. It has the appearance of *tofu*, the Chinese bean curd. The cheese is made by introducing a sour substance into milk which separates the curds from the liquid whey. The curds are then collected and excess water is allowed to drain out, leaving you with *panir*. The curdling agent that works best for me is a mixture of lemon juice and yogurt although just lemon juice alone is enough to curdle the milk. Do not fear if the *panir* appears to be falling apart; in actual use it is pressed into desired shapes before being cooked.

Pour the milk into a pot that is large enough to allow the milk to foam up freely while it boils. Heat over a medium heat stirring occasionally. While you are waiting for the milk to boil prepare the curdling agent by mixing together the lemon juice and yogurt. Now prepare a sieve or large strainer by lining the inside with two thicknesses of cheesecloth. Prop the lined sieve or strainer so that it rests firmly in a bowl with some room between the bottom of the sieve and the bottom of the bowl. By this time the milk should have begun to boil. Allow the milk to boil thoroughly until it rises to the top edges of the pot. Turn off the heat and immediately add the yogurt and lemon-juice mixture and mix thoroughly with a wooden spoon. Almost instantly you will witness the dramatic separation of the milk into the sponge-like *panir* and the thin watery whey. If the milk curd does not separate even after a minute or two, boil the mixture once more. The whey will be near the bottom of the pot and the *panir* will be floating on the top. Bring the pot over to the sieve and pour the curdled milk through both the cheesecloth and sieve. The whey will pass through and be collected in the bowl while the *panir* will remain in the cheesecloth. Save the whey to prepare other dishes such as rice, *dal* or the *matar panir* that is described in the next recipe. When the *panir* has cooled so that it can be handled, draw up the 4 corners of the cheesecloth so as to trap the *panir* within the cheesecloth. Tie the corners together so that the *panir* can hang suspended by the tied ends. Tie a string tightly around the 4 corners of the cloth just above the *panir* so that the cloth is pressed tightly against the *panir*. Let the excess water drain from the suspended *panir* for 1 to 1-1/2 hours. At the end of this time take the *panir* and cheesecloth down and transfer the *panir* to a clean dry bowl. Knead the *panir* gently but thoroughly until it forms a nice firm ball. If the *panir* is not to be used immediately, it should be placed in a plastic bag and refrigerated. The *panir* will keep for 3 or 4 days when refrigerated.

Milk

MATAR PANIR (PEAS AND CHEESE)

1 cup panir balls (see previous recipe)
1 cup vegetable oil
1 cup fresh shelled peas
or 1-1/2 cups drained canned peas
1/2 cup finely chopped onion
1/2 cup finely chopped tomatoes
1/4 teaspoon garam masala*
1/4 teaspoon coriander powder
1/4 teaspoon turmeric powder
2 cloves finely chopped fresh garlic
1/4 teaspoon cayenne (optional)
3 tablespoons ghee* or clarified butter
1 teaspoon salt.
1-1/2 cups panir whey (see previous recipe) or water
(Use only 1 cup of whey if
    canned peas are used)
1 teaspoon sugar (optional)

*see glossary

Used tofu - excellent

58

This dish is roughly translated as peas and cheese. The first step is to prepare the *panir* according to the preceding recipe. Knead the *panir* on a smooth surface for about 7 minutes. When kneading the finished *panir* into a firm round ball it is best to use the heels of your palms to push the cheese into firmness. When the *panir* is ready, break off grape-sized pieces and gently roll into small round balls using the hollows of your palms. Finish making all the *panir* balls you will need. Heat the cup of oil in a wok or any suitable pot over a moderate heat. When the oil is hot, so that a bit of *panir* when placed in the oil begins to bubble, gently place 7 or 8 of the *panir* balls in the oil for deep frying. Fry them until they turn a light golden brown which takes only a few minutes. Remove the *panir* balls from the oil using a slotted spoon that allows the oil to drain back into the pot. Now place the *panir* on absorbent paper towels to remove any excess oil and set aside.

Using a large frying pan (the heavy iron ones are the best) heat up the *ghee* or clarified butter over a *low heat*. Add the chopped onion and brown, stirring constantly with a wooden spoon. When the onion appears soft and browned, add the chopped tomato and cook for 10 minutes, stirring occasionally. The tomatoes when cooked will turn into a pulp-like sauce. Now add the garlic, *garam masala,* salt, turmeric and coriander powder and blend these into the cooked tomatoes and onions until they are well mixed. Now add 1/2 cup of the *panir* whey or water to the frying pan and simmer over a medium heat for 5 minutes. Then add the peas and stir with a wooden spoon. Add the rest of the whey (use only 1/2 cup if canned peas are used), cover and cook for 10 to 15 minutes, checking to make sure the peas are sufficiently cooked. The fresh peas take a little longer to cook than the canned peas. If you find that the fresh peas are still not cooked and there is no liquid left in the pan, add some more whey or water and cook a little longer. When the peas are cooked, add the *panir* balls and gently stir the mixture, being careful not to break any of the cheese balls. Cook uncovered for another 5 minutes so that the sauce in the pan gets absorbed into the *panir*. Check the taste of the sauce and correct the seasoning by adding more salt if necessary. If more of a hot taste is desired, the optional cayenne should be mixed in at this point. If the flavor is a bit sharp from the tomatoes, then the sugar should be added to correct this. Serve the *matar panir* hot as a main dish with rice or *parotha* (page 150).

Serves Two

Milk

YOGURT

1 quart milk
1 tablespoon yogurt
1 cup instant milk powder (optional)

Once you find out how easy it is to make yogurt you may never again want to spend money on the commercially available yogurts, some of which are made with "fillers" in place of milk. All that is needed to make yogurt is some milk and a spoonful of yogurt to begin the culture. Once you have made yogurt you will have the necessary starter for the next batch of yogurt, unless you finish it, in which case you have to start all over again.

It is important to remember, however, that while the yogurt is forming it is very temperamental and very easily affected by the temperature and humidity of the weather outside. For example, if it is a clear, sunny day outside the yogurt culture will grow quickly to produce a thick, creamy yogurt that appears as if it could be cut with a knife. On the other hand if the weather is damp, raining or heavily overcast, the yogurt may not turn out perfectly; the resulting culture may be thin and watery and not sour enough. As a rule you need more yogurt to start the culture on cold days than on hot days. The temperature also determines the length of time that is necessary for the yogurt to be fully formed. On hot days yogurt can be prepared at room temperature in 8 or 10 hours, whereas on cold days the yogurt will have to be placed in some warm spot for as long as 14 to 16 hours.

In the ingredients I have included instant milk powder as an option. Adding this milk powder will make the yogurt extra thick and creamy without adding to the yogurt's butterfat content. When the milk powder is used, it should be stirred into the cold milk before cooking, without dissolving it first in water.

First bring to boil the quart of milk (and milk powder, if used) in at least a 2-quart or larger saucepot. As the milk begins to boil, it will foam and rise to the top of the pot. If you are not watching carefully, it will boil over and make a terrible mess. The instant the milk foams to the top of the pot, it should be removed from the heat. After the milk has boiled it should be allowed to cool naturally, without the aid of refrigeration, to between 105° and 110° (a roast thermometer is helpful here). Now take 1/2 cup of the warm milk and place it in a bowl. Add to this the tablespoon of yogurt and mix well with a fork until all the yogurt is dissolved into the milk. Add this mixture to the pot of warm milk and stir once. Now transfer the milk and yogurt mixture to a thick-walled vessel of stainless steel, glass or ceramic with a lid.

Place the covered vessel on a shelf or warm corner of a room where it will not be disturbed or shaken. It is very important that the yogurt is not shaken in any way while it is forming, or the resulting product will be something less than solid. The yogurt will take about 12 hours or more to form at room temperature, depending on the weather conditions as mentioned previously. In cold weather some people place the vessel near (not on) a heat source such as a radiator, or in an oven with only the heat of a 75-watt bulb to warm the air. In the latter cold-weather technique the yogurt will be ready in 6 to 8 hours. In warm weather it is most advisable to use only the room temperature as the resulting yogurt is sweeter. I usually begin the yogurt at about 8 o'clock in the evening so that the culture can grow overnight with less chance of being disturbed. If it is a cold evening, it may take until noon the next day before the yogurt is ready. At the expected time of completion the yogurt should be gently uncovered and inspected to determine whether or not it is ready. If it has formed a solid jello-like consistency it is

ready; if it hasn't, the vessel should be recovered and without shaking, returned to its place for another hour or so until it is ready. Place the yogurt in the refrigerator after it is ready, and it will keep for almost a week. Be sure to save a tablespoon or two so that you can prepare it again without having to purchase more yogurt for a starter.

When yogurt is served with an Indian meal, it is either served in individual dishes or a portion of it is placed right on the plate or *thali*. The *thali* is a type of tray, usually made from brass or stainless steel, that serves as an individual's eating area and food container. The yogurt has many functions in the Indian meal. One is to act as a cooling agent to counteract the fiery properties of many chutneys and heavily spiced vegetables. Another important function of the yogurt is to act as a binding agent for the rice and vegetables, to facilitate eating with the fingers. In some parts of India, notably the South, the people form small balls out of their food with the help of the yogurt so that the food becomes conveniently packaged as it is eaten. I am sure that once you begin to enjoy yogurt with your meals you will find the plain, natural yogurt to be finer tasting than the fruit and syrup-laden yogurt that is so popular in the West.

Milk

YOGURT CURRY OR KADHI

2 cups sour yogurt
or 2-1/2 cups buttermilk (store-bought thickness)
3 tablespoons besan (chick-pea flour)*
2 teaspoons salt
1/2 teaspoon turmeric powder
1/8 teaspoon cayenne
1/4 teaspoon cumin powder
1/4 teaspoon coriander powder
1 teaspoon peanut oil
1 whole dried red chili pepper, seeds removed
1/4 teaspoon black mustard seeds
2 cloves garlic, chopped
pinch of hing* (optional)
2 tablespoons sugar
1/2 cup shelled roasted unsalted peanuts (optional)

*see glossary

I believe the word "curry" originated from the Britisher's mispronunciation of this dish called *kadhi*. Now all Indian dishes in the West are called curries. But this delicious hot and sour soup is the original one and the only one deserving the name curry. *Kadhi* takes about an hour to prepare but the time spent is well rewarded. It is important that the soup be cooked over a low flame and stirred constantly while it is cooking, to keep the yogurt or buttermilk from separating out of the soup. This soup is prepared at times with roasted peanuts which add an interesting crunch.

Using a fork or an egg beater, mix together the yogurt or the buttermilk with 1 cup of water. Place this mixture in a large pot along with 7 cups of water, and heat over a low flame for 5 minutes, stirring constantly. Now in a bowl mix the *besan* with 1/2 cup of water until all the flour has dissolved into the water. Add this *besan* mixture to the pot and continue to stir. Add the salt and continue to cook over a low flame for 15 minutes stirring every 2 or 3 minutes. If you neglect to stir the soup enough, the flour will mix with the yogurt to form small lumps, so be careful. After the soup has cooked a total of 20 minutes, add the turmeric, coriander, cumin and cayenne. Turn the heat up a bit and cook uncovered for another 25 minutes stirring constantly.

At the end of this cooking time the soup should have cooked down to half its original volume and begun to thicken somewhat. At this point it is ready for the final touch. Turn the heat off and let the soup stand. In a small pot or saucepan heat 1 teaspoon of peanut oil. Add the mustard seeds, chopped garlic and the whole chili pepper. When the mustard seeds begin to pop and the chili turns a deep dark brown, add the *hing*. Immediately add this hot-flavored oil to the soup and quickly cover. Keep covered for 2 minutes, then remove the cover and stir the soup well. Add the sugar and stir again. Now taste the soup and correct the seasoning. Heat up the soup over a low-to-medium flame for 5 minutes until the soup is sufficiently hot. Stir once again and the soup is ready to serve. Although *kadhi* is traditionally served with *khichadi* (page 113) or *upma* (page 39), it can be served alone or with any other dish you desire.

SHRIKHAND

8 cups plain yogurt
4 whole cardamom pods (green or white)
1/2 cup pistachio nuts, chopped
2 pinches ground nutmeg
1 cup white sugar
1 teaspoon rose water (optional)

Shrikhand is a rich sweet dish that is somewhat like custard or ice cream and would be considered a dessert in the West, but in India it is eaten as a main dish. *Shrikhand* is usually prepared for feasts or special festivals and is traditionally served with the balloon-like breads called *puris* (page 156). Made with thickened yogurt, this dish is a special treat that is known for its richness and silky smooth consistency.

In a piece of double-wrapped cheesecloth or a piece of thin muslin, suspend the yogurt over a bowl in the sink so that all the liquid drains off. Firmly tie a string around the 4 corners of the cloth above the yogurt. Allow the water to drip for 5 hours, although a longer amount of time will produce a thicker *shrikhand*. The water that has drained from the yogurt can be used to cook rice or to make one of the different *dals*. After the specified amount of time take the yogurt down and place in a bowl. The yogurt should appear very thick and about half its original volume. Lightly beat the yogurt with a fork until it becomes quite smooth. Now with the aid of a rolling pin, grind the inner seeds of the cardamom pods. Add the ground cardamom, chopped pistachio nuts, nutmeg and sugar to the beaten up yogurt. Mix very well with a spoon until all the sugar is completely dissolved into the yogurt. Taste the *shrikhand*; if it tastes too sour, add some more sugar, but not so much that it becomes overly sweet. Add the rose water and mix again. Put some whole pistachio nuts over the top of the *shrikhand* and chill for half an hour or more before serving.

Serves Four to Six

Vegetable Dishes

Many of my American friends who have become vegetarians have gone through a similar experience of becoming more aware of vegetables. They say that they are more conscious of the different vegetables, their tastes and the different methods of preparing them. It would seem that the change of diet has caused a reawakening of the taste buds of these people. It has also been brought to my attention that many people in America were weaned on canned peas, carrots and corn as their major introduction to the world of vegetables. And for the most part these canned vegetables were the main vegetable source for these people during their years of childhood. Many children grew up disliking vegetables because they were forced to eat poor-tasting, nutrition-lacking, canned vegetables, while being told that vegetables were important for their health. Vegetables became like some bad-tasting medicine that you had to take.

These same people are now extolling the virtues of vegetables because they have begun to eat and prepare them in an entirely different manner. They have realized the great difference between fresh and canned or frozen vegetables. They have begun to understand why boiling vegetables not only destroys the succulent tastes but also greatly reduces the nutritional content. Many people are even starting to see the relationship between the taste of the vegetable and how it was grown; whether the plants were picked too early or whether the type and method of fertilizing was designed to just grow the plants rapidly or to produce the most succulent vegetable. It can be said with all honesty that the process of becoming

a vegetarian has made many people more aware of the foods they are eating.

Most of India's people are vegetarians, meaning that they do not eat any flesh whether it be from a cow, fish or fowl. And since milk and dairy products are not abundant enough to satisfy the needs of the populace, vegetables constitute the major foodstuff in the diet of India's vegetarians. Every town in India has a large produce market where from sunup to sunset almost endless varieties of vegetables are displayed. Early in the morning, throughout India, you will find many ladies clad in gaily colored *saris* bargaining with great determination with the merchants over the cost of this or that vegetable. Occasionally a cow or goat will sneak its head in among the ladies to snatch away an eggplant or head of cabbage, much to the chagrin of the merchants. Small children will be nearby pretending to cry so that a sympathetic merchant will offer them a fruit to dry their tears. Arguments and discussions abound, tears and laughter ring out through the market. It is quite a colorful scene charged with energy and emotion. In India it is as entertaining to purchase the vegetables as it is to cook and serve them.

For most noon or evening meals in India only one or two vegetables are prepared. But on holidays or when guests come for dinner, you can expect the meal to include at least three or four separate vegetable dishes to be served along with the *dal* (cooked lentil). When I was a little girl, my grandmother would sometimes put me to sleep with a bedtime story. My favorite story included a lavish dinner that was served with "32 types of

Vegetables

sweets and 33 different vegetable dishes." Such is the importance of vegetables in the Indian vegetarian's diet.

These days in many Indian cities sweets can be bought ready-made, but the preparation of different vegetable dishes remains every cook's secret. A cook will always have a certain individual touch that will distinguish his or her favorite vegetable preparations from the traditional method of preparation. In my recipes I have included the traditional methods of preparing certain vegetables along with some of my own special touches and ideas. I have also given recipes for some non-Indian vegetables, such as mushrooms and celery, in place of the Indian vegetables that are not available in the West.

As much as possible I avoid using canned or frozen vegetables, as there is no real substitute for freshness. Sometimes I use canned peas when fresh peas are out of season with fairly good results. Most of the vegetables that are used in the following recipes can be bought in most grocery stores, some are available only in farmers markets or in ethnic food stores in Chinese or Mexican neighborhoods. Shop around and become familiar with the different areas and stores where fresh produce can be bought. Try not to be restricted by just what is available in your local store. In many cities in North America the variety of vegetables available is quite large, depending, of course on the different seasons. Following is a list of some familiar and not-so-familiar vegetables that are available in many parts of America along with a description of their special qualities and some tips on how to select them.

CAULIFLOWER

This vegetable is known throughout the world and is very popular in India. In most recipes the cauliflower should have its thick stem removed before it is cut up. Try to select a cauliflower that is as white as possible; yellowing can indicate that the vegetable is old. The individual flowers should appear tightly compacted which indicates proper time of picking and insures better cooking qualities.

EGGPLANT

This is probably the most popular and widely used vegetable in India. Even in a small market you will see countless varieties of eggplant in different shapes, shades and even colors. In the West the two most popular varieties are the round, globular kind and the smaller, long, thin "Japanese" variety, which is sometimes sweeter than the larger type. The best eggplants are those that have few or no seeds. The appearance of a large number of seeds in the eggplant when it is opened indicates that the plant was left to grow too long and there is a tendency for these eggplants to taste bitter and be tough. Selecting a good eggplant is sometimes difficult as most appear quite similar on the outside. Try to pick one that is neither too soft nor too hard and seems to be fresh.

OKRA

This is also known as ladies' fingers and is a popular soul food item in America. Okra look like small green swords that when cooked properly are simply delicious. Many people avoid cooking okra because, if not cooked properly, they turn out stringy or pasty. Okra is one vegetable that should not be used in a stew with other vegetables. The best okra is the small firm bright green kind. The large okra tends to be overly tough and should be avoided.

OPO (GHIYA OR BOTTLE GOURD)

This sweet-tasting squash is also called *doodhi* in India. *Opo* are fairly large vegetables with a light green, smooth outer skin, as distinguished from the rough-skinned Chinese *opo*. A large opo can weigh two pounds or more. The shape of this vegetable is something like a large cucumber with one end being thin and the other end being bulbous. This is a popular vegetable among Philippine people and is also used in Chinese cooking. In California *opo* is even sold in some supermarkets as a regular item. The way to test an *opo's* freshness is to push a fingernail against the skin. If it is fresh, your nail will easily penetrate the surface.

Vegetables

CHINESE OPO (GHEESODA)

This cucumber-shaped, rough-skinned green vegetable is called *gheesoda* in India and Chinese *opo* in oriental grocery stores. The rough skin should be entirely scraped off before cooking. The *gheesoda* should be firm and fresh looking, not limp or soft. I have seen this vegetable sold in Chinese, Japanese and Philippine neighborhood stores.

KARELA (BITTER MELON)

This vegetable is sometimes called bitter melon or bitter squash. As the name implies, it is very bitter, but only when uncooked. When cooked with certain spices, the unique flavor of the *karelas* becomes transformed into a delicious pungent taste. This vegetable is available mostly in Chinese neighborhood stores.

ZUCCHINI

This popular vegetable is very similar in looks and taste to the Indian vegetable *galka*. Looking like thin cucumbers, zucchini is available in most parts of North America. A very fine-tasting vegetable that is especially popular with Italian cooks, zucchini should be firm and not too large to insure freshness.

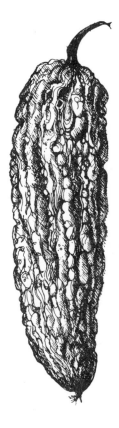

Vegetables

SOME NOTES ON COOKING VEGETABLES

In India *subji, shak* or *bhaji* all mean cooked vegetables. These preparations of cooked vegetables are called "curries" in the West. The Indian methods of cooking vegetables can roughly be divided into four groups. The first or "wet" method is for producing vegetables in a sauce, the second is the dry method of cooking vegetables, the third is for stuffed vegetables and the fourth deals with vegetables cooked with *dal*. The fourth method will be covered more completely in the chapter on *dals*.

In the wet method, vegetables are first sautéed in oil and then with the addition of some water allowed to cook to produce a sauce. This method is essentially a low-heat method of cooking.

The second or dry method involves first sautéeing the vegetables in some oil and then cooking without water over a moderate or high heat. The result is called *suki bhaji* or dry vegetables.

In the third method vegetables are stuffed with *masala* (spices) and sometimes *besan* (chick-pea flour) and allowed to cook over a low heat with the addition of some water. This method of cooking produces a rich, thick sauce.

The fourth method involves cooking vegetables together with a *dal* (a soup made from different lentils). This is a popular way of preparing vegetables in Southern India.

There are also some other methods of cooking vegetables that will be covered in other chapters such as cooking vegetables and rice together (chapter eight) or cooking vegetables in batter (chapter three).

Almost all the different ways of preparing vegetables have one thing in common, the *vadhar* or the sautéing of the vegetables in oil or *ghee*. In all the recipes in this chapter there is a step that calls for adding mustard seeds, onion or garlic to hot oil or *ghee*. When these items have sufficiently been heated the next step is to add the vegetables. This should be accompanied by a loud sound caused by the cold, moist vegetables meeting the hot oil. This "chhuum" sound is a very familiar sound in any Indian kitchen and is important to the success of the dish being prepared. Only when this sound is quite evident will you be sure that the important sautéing process is being done correctly. If you are not getting this sound, chances are that the oil is not hot enough. But if you do hear the all-important sound, you can be sure that you are on the proper path to an authentically cooked Indian meal.

Rasedar Shak/Vegetables with Sauce

Vegetables with Sauce

EGGPLANT WITH BOILED POTATOES

2 medium-size potatoes
1 medium-size eggplant (about 1 pound)
1/2 teaspoon garlic chutney (see page 51)
3 tablespoons vegetable oil
1/2 teaspoon black mustard seeds*
pinch of hing* (optional)
1/2 teaspoon turmeric powder
1-1/2 teaspoons salt
1 tomato, chopped
2 teaspoons fresh lemon juice

*see glossary

Place the whole, unskinned potatoes in a large pot of boiling water and cook until tender. Remove the potatoes when a fork easily pierces them and then peel off the skin. Chop the cooked potatoes into large cubes and set aside.

Prepare the eggplant by cutting off the top green part and then slicing into cubes about the size of the potato cubes or a little smaller. Put the cubed eggplant in a bowl of cold water so that it does not discolor while waiting to be used. Drain before using.

Prepare the garlic chutney by thoroughly grinding together the chopped garlic, coriander, cumin and cayenne with a rolling pin or mortar and pestle. After the chutney is ground into a smooth paste, remove 1/2 teaspoon and store the rest in the refrigerator.

Heat the oil over a moderate flame and add the mustard seeds. The small black seeds will begin to pop in the hot oil. When they have stopped popping, immediately add the *hing* (optional), potatoes and the well-drained eggplant pieces. Mix these vegetables together with a wooden spoon for about a minute, then mix in the turmeric and salt. Sauté this mixture for 5 minutes so that all the turmeric is well blended into the vegetables. Mix in the garlic chutney with the wooden spoon. Then add 3/4 cup water, cover and cook for 15 minutes over a low heat. At the end of this time, check to see whether the vegetables are thoroughly cooked and if there is a sufficient amount of sauce. If you feel that the vegetables are not soft enough, cook for another few minutes until they are ready. If there is little or no sauce left, then add another 1/4 cup water, stir and cook for a minute or two. Turn off the heat when the vegetables are completely cooked and add the chopped tomato and the juice of a freshly squeezed lemon. Stir and cover for a few minutes before serving. The vegetables should be hot when served so try to coordinate the rest of the meal around the cooking of the vegetables.

Serves Four

Vegetables with Sauce

EGGPLANT AND POTATOES (VARIATION)

Same ingredients as eggplant with boiled potatoes.

It is surprising to some people how an Indian cook can use the same ingredients and spices and create totally different dishes. The subtleties of a highly evolved art of cooking allow these variations. Here is a recipe that employs almost the exact items as the preceding recipe for eggplant and potatoes but the resulting dish is quite different.

First choose a good eggplant then remove the green part where the stem meets the eggplant. Cut the eggplant into cubes or sections about 2 inches long and set aside in a bowl of cold water to prevent discoloring and drying. Scrape rather than peel the potatoes clean, cut into much smaller cubes than the eggplant and place in a separate bowl of cold water to keep the potatoes from turning brown.

In a medium-size saucepot heat the oil over a moderate flame. When the oil is hot, add the mustard seeds; when the seeds have finished popping in the oil, add the completely drained potato pieces and immediately add the turmeric. Stir the mixture well and then add 1 cup water. Cover the pot and cook for 10 minutes. Then add the well drained eggplant and stir again with a wooden spoon until the two vegetables are mixed together. Now add 1/2 teaspoon garlic chutney and 1-1/2 teaspoons salt to the pot and stir until the chutney and salt are well mixed into the vegetables. Add 1/2 cup water to the pot (a little more if extra sauce is desired) and cook covered for another 15 minutes or until the potatoes are very soft. Now add the cut up tomato and the fresh lemon juice, stir and remove from the heat. Taste the sauce and correct the seasoning if necessary. This fine dish should be served piping hot with rice, yogurt and your favorite chutney. *Chapatis* as described on page 144, are also served with this dish although they are not a necessity.

Serves Four

Vegetables with Sauce

CAULIFLOWER
WITH PARBOILED POTATOES

1/2 teaspoon garlic chutney (see page 51)
2 large potatoes (about 1 pound)
1 medium-size cauliflower (about 1-1/2 pound)
3 tablespoons oil
1/2 teaspoon black mustard seeds*
pinch of hing* (optional)
1/2 teaspoon turmeric powder
1-1/2 teaspoons salt
1 tomato chopped
1/2 lemon juiced

*see glossary

Prepare the garlic chutney as described. You will be using only 1/2 teaspoon of the chutney that is produced from the recipe; store the rest in the refrigerator for future use.

Boil the potatoes, unskinned, in a pot of water until they are partially cooked, so that they are tender but not too soft. Remove the potatoes and allow to cool before peeling them. Now cut the potatoes into cubes approximately 2 inches square and set aside.

After washing the cauliflower, cut into small flowerettes and discard the thick stem. If the cauliflower appears very tender, then the stem can be cut into cubes and cooked along with the rest of the cauliflower.

Heat the oil in a pot over a moderate flame and add the mustard seeds. When the mustard seeds have ceased popping, add the *hing* (optional), cauliflower and potatoes; stir with a spoon for a couple of minutes and then add the turmeric and salt. Sauté this mixture for 5 minutes, add the garlic chutney, stir again to blend in the chutney and then add a cup of water. Cover the pot, lower the heat and cook for 15 minutes. Check at the end of this time to see whether the vegetables are sufficiently cooked. Add an additional 1/4 cup water to the pot if all the liquid has been cooked out. When the vegetables are cooked to your satisfaction turn off the heat and mix in the chopped tomato and the lemon juice. Stir the vegetables, recover and let stand unheated for a few minutes before serving. The vegetables should be served hot but only reheat if necessary.

Vegetables with Sauce

CAULIFLOWER AND EGGPLANT

1 cauliflower
1 eggplant (about 1 pound)
4 tablespoons oil
1/2 teaspoon black mustard seeds
1/2 teaspoon turmeric
2 teaspoons salt
1/2 teaspoon garlic chutney (see page 51)
1 tomato, chopped
3 teaspoons fresh lemon juice

Cut the cauliflower into buds and discard the thick stem. Wash and drain the cauliflower buds and set them aside. Remove the green top part of the eggplant and cut into small pieces about 1-1/2 to 2 inches long and place them in a bowl of cold water.

Heat the oil in a saucepot over a medium flame and when hot add the mustard seeds. When all the seeds have popped in the oil, add the cauliflower and turmeric. Sauté, stirring with a wooden spoon for a few minutes and then stir in the salt. Now add 3 tablespoons water, cover the pot, lower the heat and cook for 7 minutes. After this time add the well-drained eggplant pieces to the cauliflower and stir together. Add the garlic chutney and still using a low heat, sauté the vegetables for 2 minutes. Now add about 1-1/4 cups water, raise the heat to medium and cook covered for 15 more minutes. Check to see whether the vegetables are tender and thoroughly cooked. If there is still a large amount of liquid in the pot, turn the heat up to high and stir uncovered for a few minutes until the liquid is mostly gone, but there is some sauce left. Turn off the heat when the vegetables are done and mix in the chopped tomato and lemon juice. Stir, taste for proper seasoning and serve hot.
Serves Four

Vegetables with Sauce

GHIYA-KA-SHAK

1 small ghiya or opo* (about 1 pound)
1 tablespoon tamarind pulp*
or a mixture of 2 teaspoons lemon juice
   and brown sugar
3 tablespoons oil
1 clove finely chopped garlic
1/2 teaspoon black mustard seeds
pinch of hing* (optional)
1/4 teaspoon turmeric powder
1 teaspoon salt
1/4 teaspoon cumin powder
1/4 teaspoon coriander powder
1/4 teaspoon cayenne
1 small tomato, chopped

* see glossary

Some ghiya or opo are very large in which case you can use half and store the other half for a few days in the refrigerator. Remove the small stem portion and peel the ghiya as you would a cucumber. Cut the ghiya into round slices about 1/2 inch in thickness and then cut each slice into four sections, or if it is a very wide ghiya, into six equal sections. Any large seeds in the center should be removed, but usually the smaller ghiya do not have big seeds. Set the ghiya aside until the next step is completed.

If fresh tamarind is being used, first remove the hard shell and the pits leaving only the soft pulp. If the already pitted and preserved tamarind is used it should be allowed to soak in a bowl of warm water for 10 minutes just prior to being used.

Heat the oil in a medium-size pot over a moder-ate flame. Add the garlic and the mustard seeds. After all the mustard seeds have popped, add the pinch of hing and then immediately add the ghiya and stir for 2 minutes. Add the turmeric and salt and sauté the ghiya for 2 to 3 minutes. Now add the water, tamarind pulp (or lemon juice and brown sugar), coriander, cumin and cayenne and mix all the ingredients together. Cover the pot and cook for 10 minutes over a moderate heat. The larger ghiya are not so tender and may take a few minutes longer to cook. When the ghiya is com-pletely cooked it should be as soft as cooked eggplant. There shouldn't be very much water left in the pot when the ghiya is finished cooking. If there is too much liquid it should be reduced by cooking the ghiya uncovered over a moderate flame for a minute or two while stirring the mix-ture. Turn off the heat, mix the chopped tomato into the ghiya, let it stand for a few minutes and serve hot.

Serves Four

GHEESODA

Same ingredients as ghiya-ka-shak except substitute 4 gheesodas* (about 1 pound) for the ghiya.

* see glossary

Scrape off the rough skin of the gheesoda using the edge of a knife. Cut the skinned vegetable into cube-like pieces about 1/2-inch long. Now cook the gheesoda exactly the same as the ghiya in the pre-vious recipe. These two vegetables taste a great deal like each other which is why they are cooked in the same way.

Serves Four

Vegetables with Sauce

GHIYA-KA-KOFTA

For Kofta:
1/2 pound ghiya (about 1/2 small ghiya)*
1 cup besan (chick-pea flour)*
1/4 teaspoon cayenne
2 teaspoons vegetable oil
1/2 teaspoon salt
pinch baking soda
1 cup oil for frying

For Sauce:
1/2 cup finely minced onion
1-1/2 cups finely chopped tomato
1/2 teaspoon finely chopped fresh ginger
3 tablespoons ghee* or clarified butter
1/4 teaspoon garam masala*
1/4 teaspoon coriander powder
1/4 teaspoon turmeric
1/2 teaspoon salt
1/4 teaspoon cayenne (optional)

*see glossary

Koftas are small cherry-sized balls made from chick-pea flour *(besan)* batter and any vegetable or fruit that can be grated such as a *ghiya*, an unripe papaya or a carrot. In this recipe the vegetable is a *ghiya* that is grated and then mixed with the *besan* to make the small *koftas* which are deep fried in oil and cooked in a spicy sauce.

To make the *koftas*, first scrape off the skin from the *ghiya* and then grate. Scoop up the grated *ghiya* in your hands and squeeze out some of the excess water. If there is too much water left in the *ghiya,* it will make the batter too thin. Now mix together the grated *ghiya* and the *besan* in a bowl until a fairly thick, sticky dough is formed. Mix into this batter the cayenne, vegetable oil, salt and baking soda. Moisten the palms of your hands with some oil and proceed to form small balls out of the batter.

Pour about a cup of oil in a pot or wok and heat over a moderate flame. Test the oil for hotness by dropping a bit of batter in the oil. When the batter immediately bubbles and rises to the surface, the oil is ready. Gently slip the *koftas* into the oil and deep fry until golden brown. Remove the *koftas* from the oil with a slotted spoon that allows the oil to drain back into the pot. Collect all the fried and drained *koftas* on a platter and set aside while you prepare the sauce.

To prepare the *masala sauce* finely mince the onion, tomato and ginger, set aside but do not mix together. In a large frying pan, heat 3 tablespoons of *ghee* over a low flame. To the heated *ghee* add the onion and ginger and stir until the onion becomes soft and brown. Now add the tomato and the rest of the spices. Raise the heat to medium and stir continuously for 5 minutes or until all the ingredients are well blended together. You should now have a pulpy sauce. To this sauce add 2 cups of water and over a high flame bring to a boil for

Vegetables with Sauce

2 minutes. Turn the heat down to low and stirring occasionally cook for 10 minutes. When the sauce seems well blended and slightly thickened add the *koftas*. Cover the frying pan and cook over a low heat for 10 more minutes. At the end of this time the *koftas* should be soft and somewhat swollen. Do not overcook or the *koftas* will swell and break. Serve this dish immediately with rice or *chapatis*. *Serves Four*

Vegetables with Sauce

BAKED EGGPLANT WITH YOGURT (OLA)

1 large eggplant (about 1-1/2 pounds)
3 tablespoons yogurt
3 tablespoons water
2 tablespoons peanut oil
1/4 teaspoon black mustard seeds
2 cloves chopped garlic
1/2 teaspoon salt
1/2 teaspoon turmeric powder
1/4 teaspoon cayenne
1/4 teaspoon cumin powder
1/4 teaspoon coriander powder

Preheat the oven at 350° Wash the eggplant and pat dry with a towel. Place the eggplant on a rack in the middle of the oven and bake for 30 to 40 minutes. When the eggplant is ready, it will appear misshapen and the skin will be very wrinkled and burnt. Carefully remove the eggplant from the oven. Put on some gloves or cover your hands with a kitchen towel so that you do not get burnt in case the eggplant breaks open while you are handling it. Then let it cool at room temperature until it can be handled without gloves. Now peel off all the skin and place the eggplant in a bowl. Mash the eggplant with a fork until it forms a smooth pulp. In a separate bowl beat together the yogurt and water until they are well blended. Set both the eggplant and yogurt aside.

In a heavy frying pan heat the peanut oil over a low flame. Add the mustard seeds and chopped garlic to the hot oil. When the mustard seeds have ceased popping, quickly add the mashed eggplant and then the salt, turmeric, cayenne, cumin and coriander. Mix the spices into the eggplant and sauté for 5 minutes. Now add the well-beaten yogurt and water mixture to the frying pan and stir for 3 minutes. Cover the pan and continue to cook over a low heat for 10 more minutes. By this time the yogurt will be well mixed in with the eggplant pulp. Taste and correct the seasoning if necessary. Serve hot with *roti* or *khichadi*.
Serves Two or Three

Vegetables with Sauce

EGGPLANT WITH SNOW PEAS
OR STRING BEANS

1 eggplant (about 1 pound)
1/2 pound fresh snow peas or string beans
3 tablespoons oil
1/2 teaspoon black mustard seeds
1/4 teaspoon chopped fresh ginger (optional)
1 clove finely chopped garlic
1/4 teaspoon each coriander powder,
    cumin powder and turmeric powder
1/2 cup water
1 small tomato, chopped
2 teaspoons fresh lemon juice

Remove the green top of the eggplant and cut into cubes about 2 inches square. Place these cubes in a bowl of cold water and set aside. If snow peas are to be used they should be washed and set aside. If string beans are being used they should be washed and cut into 2-inch lengths.

Heat the oil in a pot over a moderate flame and add the mustard seeds, ginger and garlic. When the mustard seeds have finished popping, add the drained eggplant and the snow peas or string beans. Add the rest of the spices and sauté over a moderate flame for 5 minutes. All the spices should be well mixed into the cooking vegetables. Now add the water and cook covered for 15 minutes. When the vegetables are soft and thoroughly cooked, remove the pot from this heat and add the chopped tomato and the lemon juice. Stir once, cover and let stand unheated for a few minutes before serving.
Serves Four

Vegetables with Sauce

MIXED VEGETABLES

1 cup potato cubes, about 1 inch square
1 cup eggplant pieces
1 cup cauliflower pieces
1 cup broccoli spears
1 cup sliced celery
1 cup cubed carrots
1 cup snow peas or string beans, cut up
1 cup chopped cabbage (medium-size pieces)
1 sweet pepper (green or red) finely chopped
1/2 cup chopped onion
1 large tomato chopped
2 cloves garlic finely chopped
4 tablespoons oil
1/2 teaspoon black mustard seeds
1/2 teaspoon turmeric powder
1/4 teaspoon each cumin powder, cayenne,
    coriander powder and garam masala*
1-1/2 teaspoons salt
1/2 lemon or lime

*see glossary

This is an excellent dish to serve if you have to cook for a large number of people. The dish itself contains a great variety of vegetables and is very colorful to look at. Each person is sure to get one of his or her favorite vegetables. To make larger amounts just increase the quantities proportionally.

The longest step is the preparation of all the vegetables. First wash them and cut as specified in the list of ingredients. The eggplant and potato pieces should each be kept in a bowl of cold water until their time to be cooked. Set all the other cut vegetables aside in individual bowls or piles as they will be added to the pot at different times.

In a large pot heat the oil over a moderate temperature. Add the mustard seeds, chopped garlic, onion and the fresh sweet pepper. When the onion becomes soft and reddish brown, add the well-drained potatoes and sauté for a few minutes, stirring with a long wooden spoon. Add the cauliflower pieces, turmeric and salt and continue to sauté the mixture for another 5 minutes. Add 2 tablespoons water and reduce the heat to low. Cover the pot and cook for 10 minutes. Uncover the pot and add the broccoli, string beans or snow peas, cabbage and the drained eggplant. Add all the remaining spices and stir continuously for 2 minutes so that they are well blended into the cooking vegetables. Now add 1 cup of water to the pot, increase the heat to medium and cook covered for 5 minutes. Uncover and add the celery and carrot slices. Stir all the vegetables again for another 2 minutes and if there is no liquid left in the pot add a 1/4-cup of water. Cover the pot once again and cook for an additional 10 minutes. By now all the vegetables should be completely cooked and there should be only a small amount of sauce at the bottom of the pot. Add the chopped tomato and squeeze the lemon or lime juice over the vegetables. Turn off the heat and stir the vegetables well before serving. This mixed vegetable dish should be served with lots of yogurt. Rice or any Indian bread also goes very well with it.
Serves Eight approximately

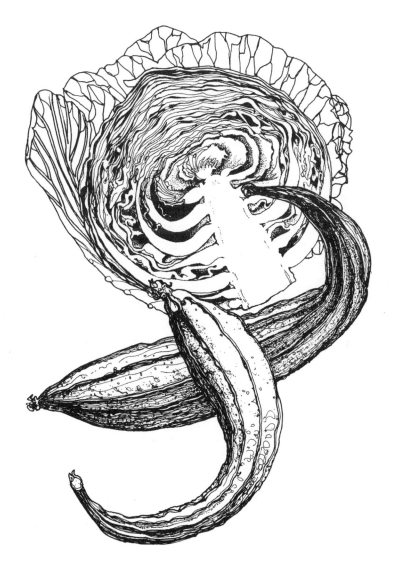

Dry Vegetables

ALU MATAR (POTATOES AND PEAS)

1-1/2 cups shelled fresh peas
2 large potatoes (about 1 pound)
1 cup chopped tomato
2 cloves finely chopped garlic
1/2 cup finely chopped scallion or onion
4 tablespoons ghee* or oil
1 teaspoon salt
1/4 teaspoon garam masala*
1/4 teaspoon turmeric powder
1/4 teaspoon coriander powder
1 cup water
1/4 teaspoon cayenne (optional)

*see glossary

Alu matar is a popular North Indian dish that means potatoes and peas. Shell the peas and set aside. Peel the potatoes and cut into sugar-cube-size pieces. Place the cut up potatoes in a bowl of cold water to prevent discoloring.

In a heavy frying pan, heat the *ghee* or oil over a low heat. Add the scallion or onion and the garlic and cook until the onion starts to turn light brown. Then add the chopped tomato and all the spices except the cayenne. Cook for 5 minutes continuously stirring to form a well blended sauce. Now add the well drained potatoes to the sauce and stir for a minute with a wooden spoon. Add the water and cook covered over a medium heat for 10 minutes. Remove the cover and add the shelled peas. Lower the heat and cook covered for another 15 minutes. At the end of this time both vegetables should be well cooked but not too soft or mushy. Taste for proper seasoning and add the cayenne if you want to increase the hotness of the dish. Serve hot with any Indian bread.

Dry Vegetables

FRIED CABBAGE WITH POTATOES

1/2 head of cabbage (about 1 pound)
1/2 cup finely chopped onion
1/4 teaspoon chopped fresh ginger
2 large potatoes (about 1/2 pound)
3 tablespoons oil
1/2 teaspoon black mustard seeds
1/4 teaspoon each cayenne, turmeric
    powder, cumin powder, coriander powder
1-1/2 teaspoons salt
few pinches garlic powder
1 tomato, chopped
1/2 fresh lemon

Shred the cabbage into coleslaw-size pieces and set aside. Carefully cut up the ginger into very small pieces. Peel the potatoes and cut into very small pieces about half the size of sugar cubes. Place these in a bowl of cold water until it is time for them to be cooked.

Heat the oil in a heavy frying pan over a medium temperature. Add the black mustard seeds and chopped onion. When the mustard seeds have stopped popping and the onion appears soft, add the drained potato pieces. Sauté the potatoes for 5 minutes, continually stirring so that they do not burn. Now add the shredded cabbage and keep stirring while you add the rest of the spices. Cook uncovered for 25 minutes, stirring the mixture every few minutes. The cabbage and potatoes will both turn golden brown when thoroughly cooked. When you feel that the vegetables are done, add the chopped tomato and the lemon juice. Stir once and it is ready to serve. This dish, however, does not have to be served immediately but can be kept warm in an oven that is set at a low temperature.

Serves Three to Four

Dry Vegetables

FRIED CABBAGE

1/2 head green cabbage (about 1 pound)
1/2 sweet green pepper, or red
3 tablespoons oil
1/2 teaspoon black mustard seeds
1/4 teaspoon each cayenne, turmeric powder,
   cumin powder and coriander powder
few pinches garlic powder (or 1 clove crushed garlic)
1 teaspoon salt
2 teaspoons lemon juice

onion, chopped

can fry partially &
  then heat off.
Heat up last minute.
Cook mustard seeds until
they pop; add onion,
peppers, garlic; then
cabbage and last the spices

1/28/95 - Very good -
can be made ahead
& re-heated
2/08 - v. & dish.
w/ mus vard sleds,
onion, tomato

To choose a good cabbage pick one that is solid and heavy for its size. Remove the worn-out looking outer leaves of the cabbage and the thick center stem. Cut the rest into fine shreds, as if preparing the cabbage for coleslaw, and set aside. Chop the pepper into fine pieces.

In a heavy frying pan, over a moderate to high flame, heat the oil. Add the chopped pepper and mustard seeds; when the mustard seeds stop popping, add all the cabbage and stir. Continue stirring while adding all the rest of the spices and the salt. Keep stirring until all the spices seem well blended into the cabbage. Cook the cabbage for another 15 to 20 minutes stirring occasionally to prevent the cabbage from burning or sticking to the bottom of the pan. When fully cooked, the cabbage will shrink down to half its original size. When the cabbage is done, remove from the heat and squeeze the lemon juice over it. Stir and taste for the correct seasoning and serve hot.

SPINACH BHAJI

2 bunches spinach
2 cloves finely chopped garlic
2 tablespoons chopped onion
1/4 teaspoon cumin seeds
3 tablespoons oil
salt to taste
few pinches cayenne
1 tablespoon lemon juice

Remove the stems and roots from the spinach and wash very thoroughly to remove any dirt or sand that might be trapped between the leaves. Drain the leaves completely and cut into medium-size pieces, as if you were cutting lettuce for a salad.

Heat the oil in a frying pan over a moderate flame. Add the garlic, onion and cumin to the oil; when the onion turns brown add the dried spinach pieces. Stir the spinach for a few minutes. Now add the salt and cayenne, raise heat and with a quicker motion stir the spinach over a high flame for 10 more minutes. By now the spinach should have shrunk into a small, dark-green mound. Stir in the lemon juice and remove from the heat. Serve the spinach immediately while it remains hot. This vegetable goes very well with rice, even to the point of pleasing many spinach haters.
Serves Three to Four

Dry Vegetables

FRIED ZUCCHINI

6 medium-size zucchini (about 2 pounds)
4 tablespoons oil
1/2 teaspoon black mustard seeds
2 chopped scallions or 2 tablespoons finely
   chopped onion (optional)
1-1/4 teaspoons salt
1/2 teaspoon each turmeric powder,
   cumin powder, coriander powder
few pinches garlic powder
or 1/2 clove minced garlic
1/4 teaspoon cayenne
1/2 fresh lemon

Carefully peel the zucchini, so as not to cut away too much of the vegetable that lies under the thin skin, and cut into fairly thin slices. In a large frying pan, heat the oil over a moderate flame and add the mustard seeds and the optional scallions or onion. When the mustard seeds are no longer popping, add the zucchini slices. Then add the turmeric and salt and begin stirring with a gentle but constant motion until all the turmeric mixes with the zucchini. If you stir too vigorously, the thin zucchinis will break and become mushy. Now add the rest of the spices while continually stirring the zucchini. Cook the zucchini, stirring every couple of minutes for another 10 to 15 minutes until they become golden brown. If the vegetable is cut into thicker slices it will take a little longer to cook. When the zucchini is finished cooking turn off the heat and mix in the fresh lemon juice. The zucchini should be served hot but can be kept warm in an oven that is set at a low temperature, for a short while.

Serves Four

Dry Vegetables

OKRA

1 pound small fresh okra
3 tablespoons yogurt
4 tablespoons oil
1/4 teaspoon black mustard seeds
pinch of hing* (optional)
1/4 teaspoon turmeric powder
1 teaspoon salt
1/4 teaspoon each coriander
    powder, cumin powder, cayenne

*see glossary

10/10/83

Excellent flavor -
not too spicy.

One thing that spoils okra is water, and so okra is best cooked without any water. You should not clean okra under direct running water; instead pat clean each okra pod with a slightly moist towel. After the okra has been cleaned in this manner remove their tops. Then cut each half lengthwise and then lengthwise again to form 4 long sections out of each pod.

In a small bowl beat the yogurt with a fork until it turns into a thick liquid. Heat the oil in a frying pan over a moderate flame. Add the mustard seeds. When they have all popped add the optional pinch of *hing*. Then immediately add the okra slices to the pan and spread them out to avoid overcrowding. Stir in the turmeric and continue stirring for 5 minutes. Add the salt and all other spices, reduce the heat to low and cook the okra for another 10 minutes, frequently shifting around and turning over the okra to prevent burning. If the okra pods are not tender or small, they should be allowed to cook a little longer. Now add the beaten yogurt to the frying pan and mix until all the okra is well coated in the yogurt. Cook for another 5 minutes or until all sides of the okra turn a yellowish brown and the sap from the okra has been cooked away. If the okra is served before it is completely cooked, it will have a somewhat sticky consistency. Okra should be served with at least one other vegetable and rice.
Serves Three to Four

GHOBI AUR MATAR
(CAULIFLOWER AND PEAS)

1 medium-size cauliflower (about 1 pound)
2 tablespoons oil
1/4 teaspoon each black mustard seeds
    and cumin seeds
1/2 teaspoon turmeric powder
salt to taste
1 cup fresh shelled peas
1/4 teaspoon cayenne
1/4 teaspoon coriander powder
1/4 cup water
2 teaspoons lemon juice

11/83

mildly spicy — very nice

This vegetable dish is easy to cook in a small wok or frying pan. First separate the cauliflower into individual small buds or flowerettes. Wash and drain the cauliflower buds and put aside.

In a small wok or frying pan heat the oil over a moderate flame. Add to the oil the mustard seeds and the cumin seeds. When all the mustard seeds have stopped popping and the cumin seeds have turned brown, add the cauliflower pieces, turmeric, and salt. Sauté the cauliflower for 5 minutes, and then reduce the heat to low and cook covered for another 5 minutes. Uncover the pot and add the shelled peas and the rest of the spices. Mix well so that all the ingredients are well blended together. Add the water, cover and cook for 10 more minutes. When both vegetables are cooked to your satisfaction remove from the heat and squeeze the fresh lemon juice over the vegetables. Mix once and serve.

Serves Four

Dry Vegetables

POTATO BHAJI

4 medium-size potatoes (about 2 pounds)
3 tablespoons oil
1/2 teaspoon black mustard seeds
1/4 cup finely chopped onion
2 cloves garlic minced
1/2 teaspoon turmeric powder
salt to taste
1/4 teaspoon cayenne
1/2 lemon juiced
2 tablespoons fresh coriander leaves*
    or 1/2 teaspoon coriander powder

*see glossary

Boil the potatoes in a large pot of water until they are tender but not too soft. Remove the potatoes from the water and allow them to cool until they can be handled by hand. When cool, peel the skin off and cut into large sections about 2 inches long. Place the potato pieces in a dish or bowl and set to one side.

Add the oil to a medium-size saucepot and heat over a moderate temperature. Add the mustard seeds, chopped onion and minced garlic. When the onions have all browned, add the boiled potato pieces, turmeric and salt. With a wooden spoon stir the ingredients in the pot until they are well blended together. Reduce the heat to a low setting and add the rest of the spices (except for the coriander leaves), while you continue stirring the mixture for a few more minutes. Cover the pot and cook for 10 minutes, stirring up the pot occasionally to reduce the chance of any burning. After this time if the potatoes are still uncooked add 2 tablespoons of water and cook a little longer until the potatoes are soft. Do not add more water or the potatoes will become soupy. Turn off the heat and mix in the lemon juice. Top with fresh coriander leaves and serve.
Serves Four

Stuffed Vegetables

STUFFED VEGETABLES

STUFFED OKRA

1 pound fresh okra
1/2 cup besan (chick-pea flour)*
1 teaspoon salt
1/4 teaspoon each coriander powder,
    cumin powder and cayenne
4 tablespoons oil
2 tablespoons water
2 tablespoons yogurt
    or 1 tablespoon lemon juice
1/4 teaspoon black mustard seeds
1 chopped garlic clove
1/2 teaspoon turmeric

*see glossary

Clean the okra by wiping with a moist towel rather than by a direct application of water, as any water hinders the cooking of the okra. Cut the tops from the okra and make a lengthwise cut to the center of the okra to form a pocket for the stuffing.

Take a large bowl and add the *besan*, 1/2 teaspoon salt, the coriander, cumin, cayenne, 2 tablespoons of oil and 2 tablespoons of water. Mix all these ingredients together with your hands. The stuffing when ready should be moist and flaky.

Fill each okra with about a teaspoon, more or less, of stuffing. Do not force the opening trying to overstuff them or they will break in half. Try to put in just the amount of stuffing that comfortably fits into each okra pod. Then set the stuffed pods gently aside. If you are using yogurt, prepare it in a separate bowl, beating with a fork until it is a smooth liquid.

Heat the remaining 2 tablespoons of oil in a large frying pan over a moderate flame. Add the mustard seeds and the finely chopped garlic. As soon as the mustard seeds begin to pop, add the stuffed okra, carefully placing them with the stuffing facing upward. Sprinkle the turmeric over a wide area of the frying pan and stir the contents gently with a wooden spoon. When the turmeric has been all blended in, reduce the heat to low and cook covered for 5 minutes. Uncover the pan and sprinkle 1/2 teaspoon salt over a large area of the pan. Stir and turn all the okra over so that all parts of the okra will be cooked equally. Add the lemon juice or the beaten yogurt to the okra and mix again. Cook uncovered for 10 to 15 minutes until the okra become golden brown. Be sure to turn and mix the okra every few minutes to prevent burning and to insure equal cooking. Serve immediately or place in a warm oven until you are ready to eat.
Serves Four

STUFFED MUSHROOMS

4 tablespoons oil
1/4 teaspoon black mustard seeds
3/4 cup besan (chick-pea flour)*
1/4 teaspoon each cumin powder,
    coriander powder and cayenne
1 finely chopped garlic clove
    or few pinches garlic powder
1 teaspoon salt
4 tablespoons water
1 tablespoon lemon juice
24 large mushroom tops

*see glossary

To prepare the stuffing, heat 2 tablespoons oil in a frying pan over a low heat. Add the mustard seeds and when they all have popped, add the *besan* along with all the spices, using only 1/2 teaspoon salt. Preferably using a wooden spoon, continually stir the *besan* until it turns a reddish color, which indicates that it is cooked. Stirring is important as the cooking mixture burns very easily. As the *besan* begins to change color, turn off the heat but continue stirring. When the cooked *besan* is cool enough to be handled, add 2 tablespoons water and the lemon juice and mix with your fingers. Break up any lumps of flour while you are mixing with your fingers. The stuffing is ready when it takes on a moist, crumbly consistency. Remove from the frying pan and store in a covered bowl until the mushrooms are ready.

Wash and drain the mushrooms, then lightly pat them dry with a paper towel. Remove the stems from the mushrooms so that a cavity is left in each top. Fill each mushroom with approximately 1/2 teaspoon of filling or as much as the cavity will hold. Place the stuffed mushrooms on a dish and put aside.

In a large, heavy frying pan heat 2 tablespoons oil over a low flame. Gently place each mushroom in the pan with the stuffing facing upwards. Try not to crowd the mushrooms too much; use two frying pans if necessary. Cook the mushrooms for 10 minutes or until the bottoms become browned. Now turn each mushroom over so that the stuffing is against the pan. If the mushrooms seem too dry, sprinkle 1 or 2 tablespoons of water over them. Cook for another 10 or 15 minutes until the stuffing side browns. Your stuffed mushrooms are now ready to be served.
Serves Four

Stuffed Vegetables

STUFFED EGGPLANT

Stuffing:
1/2 teaspoon garlic chutney (see page 51)
3/4 cup besan (chick-pea flour)*
4 tablespoons oil
1-1/2 teaspoons salt

Eggplant:
6 or 7 small "Japanese-style" eggplants
1/2 teaspoon black mustard seeds
1/4 teaspoon turmeric
1-1/2 cups water
2 teaspoons lemon juice

*see glossary

Here is a very fine dish that is a regional specialty of Western Gujarat State where I come from in India. This part of West India is also known as Kathiavad or Saurashtra, and to my knowledge this dish is not cooked the same way in any other part of India.

Prepare the garlic chutney according to the recipe. Only part of this paste will be used for this recipe. The rest of the chutney can be stored in the refrigerator for future use. In a large bowl mix 1/2 teaspoon of the prepared chutney with the *besan* by rubbing the chutney in with your fingers. Add 2 tablespoons oil and 1/2 teaspoon salt to the flour and mix with your hands until you have a stiff, lumpy consistency. Put this stuffing aside.

Wash the eggplants and remove the green top portion from each one. If the eggplants are more than 5 or 6 inches long, they should be cut in half to form 2 equal-size pieces (do not cut in half lengthwise but through the wide center). Then slice each half or whole eggplant halfway through lengthwise so that each one has a sort of pocket where the stuffing will go. Fill each eggplant piece with about a teaspoon of the stuffing and set them aside. Do not fill so much that the stuffing will fall out easily when the eggplants are cooked.

In a medium-size pot heat the remaining 2 tablespoons of oil over a low temperature. Add the mustard seeds and when they have finished popping, carefully add the eggplants. Then add the turmeric and gently stir with a wooden spoon. Cover the pot and cook the eggplants for 6 or 7 minutes, occasionally shaking the pot so that the oil will coat each one. Uncover the pot and add the water and 1 teaspoon of salt, recover and cook over a low temperature for 15 more minutes. Shake the covered pot every 5 minutes during this cooking time. Don't be concerned if some of the stuffing falls to the bottom of the pot. It will combine with the water to make a really delicious, thick sauce. At the end of the cooking time taste some of the sauce and correct the seasoning if necessary. Add the lemon juice. Stir for the last time and serve.

Serves Four

Stuffed Vegetables

STUFFED KARELAS (BITTER MELONS)

Karelas:

6 to 8 karelas (also known as bitter melon,
   bitter squash and bitter gourd)
few teaspoons salt

Stuffing:

1 pound potatoes
4 tablespoons oil
1/4 cup chopped onion
1/4 teaspoon turmeric powder
1/4 teaspoon salt
1/4 teaspoon cumin powder
1/4 teaspoon coriander powder
1/2 teaspoon cayenne
few pinches garlic powder
1 lemon
4 tablespoons brown sugar

Karelas are most commonly known as bitter melons in the West, (see page 68) and as the name implies they have a very bitter taste. But when prepared in the proper manner they give rise to a very unusual and flavorful dish. The flavor of cooked *karela* is somewhat of an acquired taste and Indian children pride themselves in being old enough to eat and enjoy this "adult" food. My father is so fond of the bitter taste of this vegetable that he would not let my mother or myself add any sugar to it. However, most Indian cooks treat the *karelas* in various manners to offset their strong bitter taste. The following recipe calls for the addition of sugar and lemon to the *karelas* which gives them a delightful pungent flavor. It will be quite a new taste sensation for anyone adventurous enough to try this recipe.

Scrape and peel the *karelas* so that all the rough skin is completely removed. With the sharp end of a knife make a slit lengthwise in the *karela,* stopping at the inner center of the vegetable. Now scrape out the middle pulp, fibers and seeds and discard. Generously sprinkle several teaspoons of salt inside the hollow *karelas.* Do not worry about adding too much salt as it will be washed off a little later. Rub some of the salt on the outside of the *karelas* and set aside for 1 hour.

Now begin preparing the potato filling. Boil the potatoes in a pot of water until they are very soft and tender. Drain, cool and then peel off the skins. Mash the potatoes in a bowl and put aside.

Now in a small pot heat 2 tablespoons of oil and add the chopped onions. When the onions brown add the mashed potatoes, turmeric, cumin, coriander, garlic, 1/4 teaspoon of the cayenne and 1/4 teaspoon of salt. Mix this well until all the ingredients are well blended together. Squeeze about 1/3 of the lemon over the cooked potatoes and mix. The stuffing is now complete, remove from the heat and finish preparing the *karelas*.

By this time (1 hour later) the salt will have melted inside the *karelas*. Squeeze as much of the melted salt out of them as you can. Wash each *karela* under running water to further remove any salt. Now wring out each *karela*, as you would wring out a wet towel. This whole process of salting and wringing out removes much of the bitterness of this vegetable. You can repeat the washing and wringing process again. When finished, drain, dry with a towel and sprinkle 1 teaspoon of brown sugar inside each *karela*. Now stuff each *karela* with 1 tablespoon or more of the potato filling. Tie each *karela* with sewing thread to secure

the stuffing while they are cooking. The finished *karela* should look something like a fat submarine tied at the center with a piece of thread.

In a medium-size pot heat the rest of the oil over a low temperature. After waiting 5 minutes add the stuffed *karelas* and sauté them gently. Over the cooking *karelas* sprinkle another 1/4 teaspoon cayenne, 1/2 teaspoon salt and 1 tablespoon brown sugar. Then squeeze another 1/3 lemon over this and mix the ingredients by shaking the pot. Cover the *karelas* and cook for 10 minutes, still over a low heat. Now uncover the pot and sprinkle another tablespoon of brown sugar over the *karelas* and turn each one over to allow equal cooking time to all parts of the vegetable and stuffing. If there is little or no liquid left in the pot, add 2 tablespoons water. Cover the pot and cook for another 10 to 15 minutes. By now both sides of the *karelas* should be golden brown. If they still are not browned after 15 minutes, continue to cook uncovered, carefully watching that they do not burn. When done squeeze the remaining 1/3 lemon over the *karelas* and add the rest of the brown sugar. Shake the pot up to mix in the lemon and sugar. Turn off the heat, cover and let stand for a few minutes before serving.

Serves Four to Six

Rice and Rice Dishes

Rice is certainly one of man's oldest foods. There is some evidence that rice was eaten in India five thousand years ago. A few hundred years later rice became widely known in China. So important was the cultivation of rice in ancient China that the word for rice came to be the same as the word for agriculture. Rice became one of the single most important crops in all Asia, a fact that remains true to this day. It has been calculated that rice is part of the daily diet of more than half the earth's population.

In India rice is a staple food that is eaten by almost every Indian at least once a day. Great respect is accorded this grain in India, so much so, that it has become a symbolic necessity to offer rice during religious holidays and weddings. The latter custom of rice at a wedding has even survived the long journey to the the West. There is a special holiday in India that marks a certain stage in the development of a young girl into a gradually maturing woman. On this holiday called *Poshi-Punam,* all little girls throughout India are supposed to be initiated into the art of cooking rice. On this day the young girl will prepare *kheer* (see page 117), a rice pudding-like dish, for her little brothers. This is the first time a young girl will prepare rice, but by the time she is considered a woman she will be expected to have learned how to prepare rice at least 15 different ways.

In the markets throughout India you will find hundreds of varieties of rice. The different types will be classified according to where they were grown, how long they were grown, what color they are and finally, the nature and description of their texture. Even in remote villages and small towns a grain merchant will display at least 6 varieties of rice, each a different quality and price. The type of rice that is considered to be one of the highest quality in India is called *basmati* rice. To eat this long, thin, hulled rice is the dream of many Indians who cannot afford its extremely high price. *Basmati* rice has a delicious nut-like flavor and a savory fragrance. In India they say that if you are cooking *basmati* rice, all the neighbors will smell the fragrance and know that you are celebrating some special occasion. *Basmati* rice is available in this country in stores that sell Indian foodstuffs and through the mail order food shops listed at the end of the book.

Brown rice, or rice that has been hulled but the light brown bran left on, is a less popular variety of rice in India. Even though the brown rice is more nutritious, the white rice is preferred because of its color and superior cooking qualities. Brown rice tends to be a little sticky when cooked and is used only in certain dishes, notably *khichadi* which is described on page 113.

Although most people think that all white rice is the same, as far as being deficient in nutrients, it really depends on the way that the rice is processed. In most countries in the West and to a certain extent in the East, rice that has been sent to a mill to be scraped and polished, loses most of the minerals and vitamins that are found in the bran and in the outermost layer of the rice. But the rice that has been hand-pounded to remove the bran still retains much of the nutrients.

Hand-pounding rice is still the method of prepar-

Rice

ation in many of the villages in India. Mahatma Ghandi stressed the importance of eating the hand-pounded rice but unfortunately the great profits to be made in large industrialized mills are slowly winning out.

In the United States rice is classified by the size of the grain and how it was processed. The three sizes of rice available are long grain, medium grain and short grain. The long-grain rice is best in most recipes as it produces a more fluffy consistency. The medium- and short-grain varieties are best used in the preparation of *khichadi* and rice batter for *dosa* (see page 42). Medium-grain rice can be used in place of long-grain rice with fairly good results if the rice is cooked over a very low heat. Brown rice as mentioned before is rice that has had only the hard outer husk removed but the second outer coat of bran is left on. This rice is the most nutritious and often very inexpensive. Regular milled white rice is available in different sizes and is very low in nutritional content.

A third variety of rice has been processed by a method known as parboiling. I believe that this parboiled or converted rice is the best white rice available in North America. The process of parboiling relocates some of the nutrients from the outer part of the rice into the center part of the grain. The rice goes through a final process of steaming under great pressure, which seals the nutrients in the rice so that the minerals and vitamins are not passed out to the water during cooking. The product is a pearly white, fluffy rice that is much higher in nutrient value than its white, machine-milled counterpart. Parboiled rice, such as Uncle Ben's, cooks in the same amount of time as ordinary white rice and should not be confused with the precooked instant varieties that take only a few minutes to cook and are lacking in taste and food value.

Different types of rice call for different cooking times and varying proportions of water to rice. Also, the age of the rice and the degree of softness of the water cause variations in cooking. Many times it is necessary to cook the rice a first time in order to find out the best way to cook it thereafter.

COOKED WHITE RICE

1 cup white rice
2 cups water
1 teaspoon salt
1 tablespoon butter

This is the basic recipe for cooking rice. Without too much difficulty you should be able to produce perfect, fluffy, non-sticky rice every time. This recipe applies to the different sizes of white rice as well as to the parboiled and converted varieties. If you purchase rice in a package, carefully follow the recipe on the package. Cook any white rice that is bought from bulk or that comes without cooking instructions in the following manner.

Some rice comes covered with a talc-like powder which makes the rice look whiter to the purchaser. This powder must be removed before cooking the rice. Rinse the rice thoroughly under running water until the water is clear. Some packaged rice, such as the parboiled Uncle Ben's are not dusted with powder and therefore do not need to be washed off before cooking. After washing the rice drain off all the water.

Bring the water to a boil in a large pot. Add the salt, stir and add the drained rice. Now add the butter, stir and cover with a tightly fitting lid. Reduce the heat to a fairly low temperature and cook for 20 minutes. At the end of this time remove the cover and check to see if the rice is ready. If the rice is not yet completely cooked and there is no water left at the bottom of the pot, add 4 tablespoons of warm water and cook covered for another 5 to 10 minutes. When ready the rice should feel soft and fluffy. If some other hot dish is to be served over the rice, such as a *dal* or a vegetable with sauce, the rice may be allowed to stand for awhile and cool slightly before being served.

Serves Four

Rice

BROWN RICE

1 cup brown or natural rice
2-1/2 to 3 cups water
1 teaspoon salt
1 tablespoon butter

Brown rice requires a longer cooking time than white rice. Most varieties require at least 45 minutes of cooking over a low flame. The light brown and green short-grain rice, that is sometimes called natural rice, requires an hour to cook. The unique flavor of the natural rice is a pleasant change for those who eat rice daily.

To prepare the brown rice, first wash under running water and then drain. In a medium-to-large-size pot boil 2-1/2 cups of water. When the water starts boiling, add the salt and stir. Now add the rice and the butter and stir with a spoon. Leave the pot uncovered for a few minutes until the water begins to boil again. When the water starts boiling lower the heat to the *lowest* possible setting and cover. Let the rice cook undisturbed for half an hour. Then check to see how the rice is doing. If it is still very hard and appears dry, add 1/4 cup hot water and cook covered for another 15 minutes. Check again at the end of 15 minutes and if still not ready, add water if needed and cook covered for another few minutes until ready. By this time the rice should be fully cooked. The finished rice will not appear as fluffy as white rice. Stir the pot once before serving this flavorful and nutritious rice.

Serves Four

BASMATI RICE

1 cup imported basmati rice
2 cups water
1/2 teaspoon salt
1 tablespoon butter

- add 1 whole clove

For special occasions *basmati* rice is the perfect rice to serve. If you live in a city that has a large Indian population such as New York or San Francisco, *basmati* rice can be obtained in a number of stores selling Indian dry goods. If it is not available locally, it can probably be ordered from one of the mail order shops listed at the end of the book.

This rice must be washed thoroughly to remove any whitening powder that may coat it. Wash the rice under cold running water while you rub the grains with your fingers. Continue to wash until the water is clear. Drain the rice thoroughly using a colander. Now place the water and salt in a large pot and bring to a boil. When the water starts to boil, add the rice and stir with a fork. Immediately reduce the heat to low and cook covered for 10 minutes. At the end of this time uncover and check to see that all the water has absorbed into the rice. Stir the rice with a fork and add the butter. Remove the pot of rice from the heat, cover and let stand for 2 minutes. Now gently stir the rice to mix in the butter and serve the most luxurious rice in the world.

Serves Four

Rice

KESARI-BHAT (SAFFRON RICE)

1/4 teaspoon saffron threads
3 tablespoons milk
1 tablespoon butter
1/2 cup yellow raisins
1/2 cup cashew pieces or sliced almonds
1 teaspoon salt
1-1/2 cups converted rice
   or any white, long-grained rice
3-3/4 cups water for converted rice
   or 3 cups water for regular white rice
1 tablespoon sugar

Measure out the saffron threads into a bowl and crumble them into smaller pieces. Heat, but do not boil, the milk in a pot. Pour the hot milk over the saffron and let stand while you begin preparing the rice.

In a small pot or frying pan, over a low heat, melt the butter. Add the nuts and raisins to the melted butter and sauté for 2 minutes. The temperature should be set very low so that the butter does not burn. Remove the raisins and nuts and put aside.

Boil the water for the rice and add the salt to it. Add the washed and drained rice to the boiling water and stir with a fork. Lower the heat and cook covered for 15 to 20 minutes or until the rice is nearly ready but not yet done. There should still be some water remaining in the pot after the 15- to 20-minute cooking period. With the cover removed add the saffron milk mixture and the sugar. Stir the rice gently with a fork until the sugar has been well mixed in. Add the buttered raisins and nuts and stir again. Be careful while you are stirring the rice, not to break the individual grain or the rice will become mushy. By this time the rice will have taken on a light yellow color from the saffron. Cover the pot and cook for a few minutes till all the liquid has been absorbed and the rice is completely cooked. By now the color of the rice will be bright yellow and a pleasant saffron aroma will be filling your kitchen to stimulate your guests' appetites. Serve the rice immediately as it does not taste the same reheated.

Serves Four to Six

Rice

PEAS PILAU

2 tablespoons butter or ghee*
1 hot green chili
or 1/2 bell pepper, finely chopped
1/4 cup finely chopped onion
1/2 teaspoon fresh chopped ginger
4 cardamom pods
4 whole cloves
1 stick whole cinnamon
1 cup white rice (converted or
   parboiled rice preferred)
1 cup fresh or canned peas
1/4 teaspoon turmeric powder (optional)
2-1/4 cups water
1 teaspoon salt

*see glossary

Melt the butter or *ghee* in a large pot over a very low flame. When the butter has melted, add the pepper, onion, ginger, whole cardamom pods, whole cloves, and the stick of cinnamon broken into several small pieces. Continually stir this mixture from 5 to 7 minutes while regulating the heat so that the butter does not burn. When the onions are soft and transparent, add the rice and stir for 2 minutes so that all the rice gets coated with the butter and spice mixture. If fresh peas are being used, they should be added to the rice now. (Canned peas should be added later.) Stir the fresh peas in and if a yellow color is desired, the optional turmeric should be mixed in. Without the yellow coloring the dish will still appear aesthetically pleasing with the green peas and colorful spices highlighting the snow-white rice.

Continue to stir the rice and peas for 5 more minutes over a low flame. Now add the water and the salt, raise the heat slightly and bring to a boil. Now lower the heat again to its lowest setting and cover the pot. Cook for 18 to 20 minutes till all the water has been absorbed and rice is soft and fluffy. If canned peas are used, they should be drained well and stirred into the rice about 5 minutes before the rice is completely cooked.

Serve the rice with the whole spices left in, but remind your guests that they should be careful and not mistake a piece of spice for a pea.
Serves Four

RICE WITH RAISINS AND NUTS

2-1/2 cups water for converted parboiled rice
or 2 cups for plain white rice
1/2 teaspoon salt
1 cup parboiled or regular white rice
1 tablespoon butter or ghee*
1/4 cup raisins
1/4 cup chopped almonds

*see glossary

Bring the water and salt to a boil in a medium to large pot. Rinse the white rice clean under running water, drain and add to the boiling water. Reduce the temperature to low, cover and cook for 15 to 20 minutes. While the rice is cooking, heat the *ghee* or butter in a small frying pan over a low heat. When the butter or *ghee* has melted add the raisins and chopped almonds and sauté them for 6 or 7 minutes being careful that the butter or *ghee* does not burn. About 5 minutes before the rice has completed cooking, add the raisins, almonds and whatever butter or *ghee* is left in the frying pan to the pot of cooking rice. Stir all the ingredients once or twice, recover and cook for the remaining 5 minutes until the rice has finished cooking. When the rice is ready, it will appear soft and fluffy and there will be no water remaining in the pot. Remove from the heat, stir once with a fork and serve.

Serves Four

Rice

VEGETABLE BYRIANI

1 cup eggplant, cut into cubes
1 cup carrot cubes
1 cup fresh, shelled peas
1 cup cauliflower buds
1 medium-size onion, finely chopped
1 garlic clove, finely chopped
1 large tomato, finely chopped
1 green pepper, finely chopped
2 tablespoons butter or ghee*
4 whole cloves
4 cardamom pods
1 stick cinnamon 1-1/2 to 2 inches
2 cups uncooked white rice (parboiled preferred)
1/4 teaspoon cayenne (optional)
2 teaspoons salt
4 cups water

*see glossary

Cut the eggplant and carrot into smaller than sugar-cube size pieces and separate the cauliflower into small flowerettes.

In a large pot heat the butter or *ghee* over a low temperature so that it melts but does not burn. To this add the chopped onion, garlic and pepper and stir for 2 minutes. Now add the cloves, whole cardamom pods and the stick of cinnamon broken into 3 pieces. Continue to stir all the spices over a low heat until the onions brown. Then add the tomato and continue to stir for about 7 minutes. By this time the tomato pieces will have integrated with the spice mixture to form a smooth sauce. Add the rice, cayenne and salt and sauté for 2 more minutes so that the rice becomes coated and slightly fried. Now add the vegetables and stir all the ingredients so that the vegetables and rice are coated with the tomato-sauce mixture. Add the water, lower the heat, cover and let the *byriani* cook for about 20 minutes or until all the water has been absorbed. By this time the rice and vegetables should be completely cooked. In this recipe the vegetables are actually steam-cooked, which makes them very tender and delicious. The *byriani*, when served with plain yogurt, is a meal in itself. *Serves Six to Eight*

RICE WITH MUSHROOMS

3 to 4 cups cooked white or brown rice
1 cup finely sliced mushrooms
1/4 cup finely chopped scallions or onions
1 small hot green pepper, finely chopped
or 1/2 sweet bell pepper with 1/4 teaspoon cayenne
2 tablespoons peanut oil or any vegetable oil
1/4 teaspoon salt
2 teaspoons fresh lemon juice

Prepare approximately 3 to 4 cups white or brown rice according to package directions or from either the first or second recipes in this chapter. Allow the rice to cool in an open bowl for about an hour, mixing it once or twice during this time to let the bottom rice cool. If you want to quicken the process, you can put the uncovered bowl of rice in the refrigerator for 1/2 hour.

Using a large heavy frying pan, heat the oil over a low flame. Add the mushroom slices and the chopped pepper and onions. Continually stir these ingredients until the onions or scallions brown. Now stir in the cooked rice and add the salt and cayenne (if a sweet bell pepper was used). Continue to stir the rice mixture over low heat for 10 minutes so that all the ingredients are well mixed together. At the end of this time add the lemon juice, stir once again and serve.
Serves Four

RICE WITH PEANUTS

1 cup uncooked white long-grain rice
or converted parboiled rice
2-1/2 cups water
1 teaspoon salt
1/4 cup shelled, unsalted and preferably
roasted peanuts

This is an interesting rice variation. Cook the rice using the directions on the package or following this method. Boil the water in a large pot. Add the salt and when the water begins to boil, add the washed and drained rice. Cover the pot and reduce the heat to the lowest setting. Cook for around 15 minutes until the rice is nearly done and there is still some water remaining in the pot. Now add the shelled peanuts and stir the rice with a fork. Cover the pot and cook for the remaining 5 minutes or until the rice is soft and fluffy and all the water has been absorbed. Remove the rice from the heat and let stand in the covered pot for a few minutes longer. Now stir the rice with a fork to separate the individual grains and serve with any vegetable or combination of dishes.
Serves Four

Rice

COCONUT RICE

1/2 fresh coconut
3 cups water
1 cup converted parboiled rice or basmati rice*
1 tablespoon butter
4 whole cloves
4 whole cardamom pods (green or white)
1 teaspoon salt

*see glossary

The coconut is an especially important food item to the many people who inhabit the southern coastal areas of India. Ordinary crops do not grow well in these sandy, marshy areas, but here the coconut thrives. All parts of the coconut tree are used for some purpose. The leaves are used as a fuel, for the wood-starved coastal areas. Coconut oil is used for cooking and for different cosmetic purposes such as a hair conditioner. The strong outer husk of the coconut, called *coir,* is processed into a strong durable matting material. The liquid of the green coconut is used as a medicinal for sore throats and colds. And the succulent meat of the coconut is used in practically everything that is cooked by these people to give their food and sweets a characteristic coconut taste. Coconuts have a further advantage in that they can stay fresh for long periods of time and need little special care to preserve them. So important is the coconut that it is given as an offering when visiting a temple or holy place. Some coastal people even construct their houses from the long durable leaves of this beautiful palm tree.

Here is a coconut rice dish that could be served on a special occasion or holiday. Its rather long preparation makes it somewhat unsuitable for just an ordinary meal.

First purchase a coconut that when shaken, feels as though it is very full of liquid. At one end of the coconut there will be two or three soft spots. Puncture the coconut at one of these soft spots and drain out all the coconut milk. This liquid makes a most refreshing drink when cooled but is not used in this recipe. Break the coconut open using a hammer, or if you are adept with a machete, one well-placed blow will divide the coconut in two. You will only be using one-half of the coconut so you should store the unused portion in the refrigerator.

Using the blunt end of a butter knife, carefully pry the white meat loose from its hard shell. Sometimes the coconut meat separates easily from the shell in one or two pieces; other times it is necessary to pry the coconut from the shell in many small pieces. The coconut that has been separated from the shell will still have a thin brown layer on one side. This brown layer is normally edible when the coconut is eaten by itself, but for this recipe that brown layer will have to be removed, by peeling it away with a sharp knife. Now take a piece of the shelled and skinned coconut and using a sharp knife cut it into very thin strips until you have 1/4 cupful. Spread these coconut pieces onto a large frying pan and place over a low heat. Stir the coconut until the thin strips turn a light brown.

Rice

Remove the coconut from the frying pan and set aside. These browned coconut slivers will be used to top the rice dish.

Cut the remaining 1/2 coconut into small chips and pieces until you have about 1 cupful. These will be used to make a coconut milk that is different from the liquid that is contained within the coconut. In India, these coconut pieces would be mashed with a stone and then mixed with hot water, to form the coconut liquid. Using an electric blender simplifies the process. First heat the water but do not boil. Add 1 cup of the heated water to the blender along with the cup of coconut pieces. Cover the blender and mix the coconut and water for 1 minute. Stop the blender and add the remaining 2 cups of hot water and continue to blend at high speed for another few minutes. The coconut pieces should be well shredded by now and the water will have turned into a frothy milk-like liquid. Using a double layer of cheesecloth, form a pocket that will allow the coconut milk to be strained from the shredded coconut into a bowl. Pour about a cup of the liquid into the cheesecloth and firmly squeeze the liquid through until you are left with only the dry coconut shreds. Discard the coconut pulp and strain the remaining liquid that is in the blender. You will have extracted approximately 2-1/2 cups of the coconut milk. Put this in a bowl and begin preparing the rice.

If converted, parboiled rice is used, it does not have to be washed, but the *basmati* rice will have to be thoroughly cleaned to remove any talc or glucose that is used to dust the rice. Rinse the rice under cold running water until the water is clear. Drain the rice and set to one side.

In a medium-to-large-size pot melt the butter over a low heat. Then add the whole cloves and whole cardamom pods. Regulate the heat if necessary so that the butter does not burn. In 2 or 3 minutes the cloves will begin to swell. Immediately add the well-drained rice and stir until all the grains are coated with the melted butter. After 3 minutes of continuous stirring add the 2-1/2 cups of extracted coconut milk, if white rice is used, but only 2 cups if *basmati* rice is used. Add the salt.

Stir the rice and milk with a fork and cover with a tight-fitting lid. Cook over a low heat for 15 to 20 minutes if converted rice is used, or for 10 minutes if *basmati* rice is used. Stir the rice every 5 minutes so that no rice sticks to the bottom of the pot. Continue to cook the rice until only a very slight amount of liquid is left in the pot and the rice is tender but not completely soft. Turn off the heat and stir the rice with a fork. Recover the pot and let stand a full 10 minutes. The steam inside the pot will complete the cooking process. Empty the rice into a serving bowl and garnish with the fried coconut slices prepared in the beginning of the recipe. Serve this rice hot with any of the *dals* listed in the next chapter.

Serves Four

KHICHADI

1 cup brown rice or natural short-grain rice
1/2 cup mung dal (with skins)*
3-1/4 cups water
1-1/2 teaspoons salt
1/2 teaspoon turmeric powder (optional)
1 tablespoon butter

*see glossary

Khichadi (pronounced kitch-a-de) is the daily fare of many a humble Indian. It is the first solid food given to an infant and is served in ashrams across India. The reason khichadi is considered a humble food is because it is prepared with the inexpensive brown short-grain rice and because the finished product has an all-mixed-together consistency. As tradition goes in India khichadi is never served to a guest, at least not on the first day. But it is a very nourishing dish, rich in proteins, minerals and vitamins. The oldest man living in the village where I was born attributed his longevity to his daily diet of khichadi. While the name khichadi covers a variety of similar preparations, it generally means a combination of brown rice cooked together with the protein-rich mung dal. The different variations of khichadi lie in the choice of dals or split grains that are used, so that you can have chana-dal khichadi or masoor-dal khichadi just by substituting dals. Here is the basic recipe for this unpretentious but important dish.

Mung dal can be purchased with or without a thin dark skin. Traditionally khichadi is prepared with the skin still on the dal, but can also be made with the skinless mung dal. Wash the rice and dal separately and thoroughly. Drain the water from the dal and set aside. Soak the washed rice in 2 cups of water for about 1 hour. The dal should not be soaked. Add the 3-1/4 cups of water and salt to a large pot and bring to a boil. Drain the soaking rice thoroughly. Now add the rice and dal to the boiling water and lower the heat. Mix in the optional turmeric, if you desire the khichadi to turn a pleasant yellow color. Cover the pot and cook for 45 minutes over a low temperature. At the end of this time check to see whether both the rice and dal are quite soft. When the khichadi is done, it should be very soft and mushy rather than light and fluffy. If you feel that it is not sufficiently cooked and there is no water left in the pot, add a few tablespoons of water and continue to cook, covered, for another 5 to 10 minutes. Turn off the heat when done and add the butter. Cover the pot and let stand for 2 minutes so that the butter will be melted by the trapped heat. Stir the melted butter into the khichadi and serve hot with your favorite Indian bread and vegetables.

To make masoor-dal khichadi, substitute masoor dal (skinned) for the mung dal and cook as above but do not add any turmeric.

Serves Four

Rice

KHICHADI WITH BLACK-EYED PEAS

3 cups water
1 teaspoon salt
3/4 cup brown or natural rice
1/4 cup black-eyed peas
1 tablespoon butter

I came to the United States from India to attend school in Albany, New York. In Albany there were no Indian import stores or special spice shops so I had to make do with whatever local ingredients I could find. Instead of using the traditional *dals* to make *khichadi* I cooked black-eyed peas with brown rice and came up with this delicious *khichadi,* which became one of my prime Indian food substitutes.

First bring the water and salt to a boil in a large pot. Mix the rice and black-eyed peas together in a bowl and rinse clean under running water. Drain the rice and peas and add them to the boiling water. Continue to cook uncovered, over a high flame until the water begins to boil again. Then cover the pot and reduce the temperature to its lowest setting. Cook the rice and black-eyed peas for 40 to 45 minutes till both the rice and beans are soft. Now turn off the heat, add the butter, stir with a fork and cover the pot. Let the covered pot stand for a few minutes before serving.
Serves Four

Rice

CHANA DAL KHICHADI

1/4 cup chana dal (split chick-pea)*
3/4 cup brown or natural rice
1 tablespoon oil or butter
4 whole cloves
1 clove chopped garlic
1 fresh green chili, chopped (optional)
1 teaspoon salt
1/4 teaspoon turmeric powder
3 cups water

*see glossary

Look through the *chana dal* and remove any strange-looking objects such as dark-colored skins, other grains and pebbles. Mix the *dal* and rice together in a bowl and thoroughly wash under running water. Drain the rice and *dal* and put aside. In a medium-to-large-size pot, heat the oil or butter over a low temperature. Add the whole cloves, chopped garlic and the optional green pepper (for added zest). After 2 minutes or so the cloves will begin to swell and release a sweet fragrance. Immediately add the washed and drained rice and *dal* mixture. Stir with a fork for 5 minutes and then add the salt and turmeric. Stir for another 3 minutes to mix in all the salt and turmeric. Now add the water and cook covered over a low temperature for 45 to 50 minutes, until both grains are quite soft. This *khichadi* goes very well with any of the vegetable dishes described in chapter four.
Serves Four

KHEER (INDIAN-STYLE RICE PUDDING)

1 cup uncooked white long-grain rice
   (parboiled is fine)
2 cups water for cooking rice
8 cardamom pods
2 quarts milk
1 cup sugar or honey
3 tablespoons butter
1/2 cup raisins (yellow if possible)
1/4 to 1/2 teaspoon saffron threads (optional)
1/2 cup chopped pistachio nuts

Kheer is a sweet, rich dish that is especially prepared for holidays and festive occasions. Because it is both sweet and made with rice (both symbols of happiness and good fortune), *kheer* is an important part of many religious feasts and special occasions such as the *Poshi-Punam* mentioned in the introduction. Although the saffron is listed as an option, it really adds a distinctive color and taste to the *kheer*. You will be surprised at the creamy consistency and richness of this rice and milk dish. Be sure to begin the preparation of the *kheer* well in advance of the time it will be eaten, so that it has sufficient time to cool, about 2 hours.

Begin by cooking the rice in a large pot according to package direction or the recipe at the beginning of this chapter, but entirely omit the addition of any salt or butter while preparing the rice. Cook the rice in a covered pot over a low heat for 20 minutes (less time for *basmati* rice) till it is nearly done. If at the end of this time there is still a little water left at the bottom of the pot, it is all right.

While waiting for the rice to cook prepare the cardamom pods by opening the outer shell of each pod and collecting the small black seeds contained within. Discard the outer shells and with a rolling pin crush the tiny seeds.

When the rice is nearly finished cooking but not quite done, add the milk, raise the heat to medium and cook *uncovered* for 1 hour, stirring every 2 or 3 minutes. It is important to stir the rice and milk often to prevent the rice from sticking to the bottom of the pot. At the end of an hour the rice and milk will have thickened and the volume will be reduced by about one third.

Now add the honey or sugar, butter, raisins, crushed cardamom seeds and the optional saffron threads. Stir continuously for 5 minutes to thoroughly mix in the sugar or honey. Taste the *kheer* for sweetness and add more sugar or honey if you feel that it should be sweeter. Continue to cook for another 15 minutes stirring frequently so that the saffron color and taste can be equally distributed throughout the rice. Remove the pot from the heat and transfer the *kheer* into the dish in which it will be served. Top with the chopped pistachio nuts and place in the refrigerator to cool.

Kheer can be served hot, but I personally prefer it cold, so let it cool, undisturbed, for an hour or two before offering it to your guests. *Kheer* is eaten with Indian bread. Although *kheer* should be served as part of the main dish it tastes equally good as a dessert.
Serves eight with a little left over for the next day.

Rice

LEFTOVER RICE

If you have leftover white rice you can store it in the refrigerator in a covered bowl for 2 or 3 days. The formerly soft and fluffy rice will turn into a soft mass of stuck-together rice. It will not appear very appetizing and even when reheated the individual grains will stick together and be overly soft. Rice is best reheated by first gently stirring it with a fork to separate the grains and then adding 1 or 2 tablespoons water per cup of cooked rice to the pot. Place the covered pot over a very low heat and cook for about 5 minutes. A better idea is to prepare one of the following dishes that are perfect for leftover rice. They are both good-tasting and colorful to the eye, so much so that you could even serve them to guests.

VADHAR BHAT (FRIED RICE)

1 green hot chili pepper or 1/2 sweet bell pepper
1/4 cup finely chopped onion
or 2 chopped scallions
1/4 teaspoon chopped fresh ginger
1 tablespoon oil
1/4 teaspoon whole cumin seeds or jeera*
2 cups leftover cooked rice
1/4 teaspoon turmeric
2 to 3 tablespoons water
salt to taste
2 teaspoons lemon juice

*see glossary

Remove any seeds or fibers from the pepper and chop into small pieces. Heat the oil in a frying pan over a low-to-medium temperature and add the cumin seeds *(jeera)*, onion or scallions, ginger and chopped pepper. When the onions brown, add the rice and turmeric and reduce the heat to low. Sauté the rice and other ingredients, separating the grains of rice with a fork. Cook in this manner for 5 minutes continually stirring the rice. Now add 3 tablespoons of water if the rice is dry, 2 tablespoons if it is moist, add salt to taste and cover the frying pan. Cook for 5 more minutes and then remove from the heat. Add the lemon juice, stir and serve.
Serves Two or Three

LEFTOVER RICE WITH PEAS

1 cup fresh shelled peas
or 1 cup canned very young peas
2 cups (approximately) leftover cooked rice
1 tablespoon butter
1/4 cup chopped onion
1/4 teaspoon each turmeric powder,
    cumin powder, cayenne
2 teaspoons fresh lemon juice
1/4 teaspoon salt

If you are going to use fresh peas, shell them and steam cook in the following manner. Bring to a boil 1/4 to 1/2 cup of water in a small pot. Reduce the heat to very low, add the shelled peas and cover. Cook for approximately 7 minutes until the peas are soft and all the water has been cooked out. If there is any water left, simply drain it off when the peas are sufficiently cooked. The canned peas do not have to be precooked as they are already soft, but any liquid from the can should be drained off.

Separate the grains of the leftover rice by gently stirring with a fork. In a large frying pan melt the butter over a very low heat so that it does not burn. When the butter has melted, add the chopped onions and stir until they brown. Now add the rice and the turmeric and sauté for 2 or 3 minutes so that the turmeric is well mixed into the rice. Stir in the cumin, cayenne and lemon juice with a fork. Add 1/4 cup of water and the salt to the pan and stir again. Cover the pan and cook over a low heat for 5 minutes. Remove the lid and add the peas. Continue to cook the rice and peas, uncovered, for 5 minutes, stirring frequently. Serve immediately with chutney, yogurt and any Indian bread.

Serves Two or Three

Dals

Dal literally means a split lentil but the use of the word *dal* has grown to include the important soup-like preparation that is made from split or whole lentils. No Indian meal would be complete without a *dal*. In fact the most simple Indian meal is just rice and *dal*. The prepared *dal* is served in individual bowls so that each person can decide how much *dal* he wants over his rice or other food. The *dal* can also be eaten straight from the individual bowl in which it is served, much in the same manner as soup. Mostly, *dal* is eaten in a combination of these two methods.

The lentils that are available in the West can be obtained in spice stores or by mail order as explained at the end of this book. Some lentils such as *chana* can be purchased in ethnic neighborhood grocery stores under different names. The Indian *chana* is known as the garbanzo bean in Spanish-speaking areas and as a chick-pea in East European and Middle Eastern areas. Along with *chana dal* the most popularly used lentils are the split *mung bean,* which is called *mung dal,* and *toor dal,* another split grain. Sometimes you will run across a grain or lentil with which you are not familiar or that is not described in this book. These can turn out to make delicious *dals.* Try substituting one of these different lentils in one of the recipes listed. You may be pleasantly surprised.

One note of warning, all lentils should be carefully looked through to remove any foreign objects such as stones, other grains and the like. In India, women often make a social gathering when helping a friend sort out the stones and things from her supply of *dals.* This usually happens just after the harvesting of the grains. The ladies form a circle around a mound of newly picked lentils and exchange gossip, perhaps sing a folk melody and clean the *dal* all at the same time. Nothing spoils the flavor of a dish more than nearly breaking your teeth on a pebble that was left in the *dal.*

As mentioned before at least one *dal* is eaten daily by most people in India. *Dals* contribute greatly to the nutritional needs of a vegetarian diet because they are high in proteins, minerals and vitamins. The lentil is either cooked by itself to produce a soup-like *dal* or cooked with vegetables or rice to form one of the many *dal*-based dishes. Most people in India mix their rice and *dal* together when eating, although the people in Punjab take their *dal* mostly with different types of flat breads. Northern Punjabis use the wheat-based *rotis* to eat with their *dal* because that part of India is rich in wheat and has little land that is good for growing rice.

The split lentils cook in a much quicker time than the whole lentils. Split grains are also used in the West where the split green pea is a popular soup ingredient. Split green or yellow peas, in fact, can be substituted for Indian lentils when the latter are not available. The cooking process of some whole grains can be speeded up by the addition of a little baking soda while they are being cooked. Although I have heard some criticism on the nutritional soundness of baking soda, I leave it up to the individual person whether she or he wishes to use this additive. As described in the different recipes,

Dals

whole lentils sometimes call for long hours or at times days of soaking in order to soften them up sufficiently to be cooked in a reasonable length of time. The quickest *dals* to prepare are the small skinned varieties such as *mung dal, masoor dal* and *urad dal.* When preparing an Indian meal, the *dal* should be prepared first, as it is easily reheated when the rest of the meal is finished. Any leftover *dal* can be stored in a covered bowl or container in the refrigerator for 2 to 3 days and will still taste freshly made when reheated.

TOOR DAL

1 cup toor dal
6 cups water
1 teaspoon salt
pinch baking soda (optional)
1/4 teaspoon each turmeric powder, cumin
    powder, coriander powder, chopped fresh ginger
2 teaspoons vegetable oil
1/4 teaspoon black mustard seeds *Not peppercorns*
1 whole red chili pepper (dry)
1 ripe tomato
1/2 fresh lemon
1/2 hot green chili pepper, chopped (optional)
1 tablespoon chopped fresh corainder (optional)*

*see glossary

*10/18/83 - Lovely. Used
Jalapeno pepper - first
curry leaves*

This lentil is known as pigeon peas in the West, but in India this same pea when split in half is called *toor dal* and is the most widely used of all the *dals*. *Toor dal* is known also as *tur dal* or *toovar* and sometimes *arhar dal* and will be found in every kitchen in India. It is available in the West through the food stores listed at the end of this book or in any spice or grain store where Indian people shop. This split grain usually comes covered with a layer of oil which acts to preserve freshness. If the *dals* were not coated with oil, they would spoil quickly and have a very short shelf life. An oil coating is an effective way of preserving a food without the addition of questionable chemical preservatives.

The oily covering must be thoroughly removed before cooking. Wash the *dal* under very hot running water until there appears to be no oil left. Then drain all the water out and put aside.

Bring the 6 cups of water to a boil in a large pot, add the salt and stir once. Add the cleaned and drained *toor dal* to the boiling water. Wait until the water begins its second boil, then reduce the heat to medium and continue to cook for 10 minutes in the uncovered pot. Then add the optional pinch of soda to speed the cooking process. Now cover the pot and continue to cook for 30 more minutes over medium heat. At the end of this cooking time, remove the cover and add the turmeric, cumin, coriander and chopped ginger. Stir in all the spices well using a wooden spoon. Recover the pot and cook for 10 minutes; then remove the cover again and let the *dal* simmer while you prepare the next step.

Heat the oil in a frying pan over a low flame and then add the black mustard seeds and the dried red chili pepper which has been broken into 3 pieces with all seeds removed. The mustard seeds when hot will begin to pop; when they have finished popping, add the oil, seeds and pepper to the simmering pot of *dal*. This hot oil will cause a sputtering sound, but that is only natural. Immediately cover the pot for 2 minutes, then remove the cover and stir. Now add the tomato, which has been chopped into medium-size pieces, and squeeze the lemon into the pot. Stir once with a spoon and the *dal* is ready to be served. Taste and add more salt if necessary.

For additional hotness, you can add the chopped fresh green chili pepper and the chopped fresh coriander leaves to the top of the cooked *dal*. *Serves Four to Six*

Dals

CHANA DAL

1 cup chana dal (split chick-peas)
    or 1 cup yellow split peas
7 cups water
1 teaspoon salt
1/4 teaspoon each cayenne, turmeric
    powder, cumin powder, coriander powder
1 tablespoon tamarind pulp*
or 1 tablespoon lemon juice and 1 teaspoon sugar
1 tablespoon vegetable oil
1/4 teaspoon black mustard seeds
1 clove garlic

*see glossary

Indian *chana* is known as chick-peas or garbanzo beans in the West. When the *chana* is split into two equal pieces, it becomes *chana dal*. Whole chick-peas or garbanzo beans appear to be a light brown color but this is actually the color of the skin. When the *chana* is split in half and the skin removed, the *chana dal* appears yellow. *Chana dal* greatly resembles the ordinary split yellow soup peas that are commonly sold in most Western supermarkets. You can substitute these yellow split peas for the *chana dal* in this recipe and come out with a very good tasting, if not quite authentic, *dal*.

Begin by soaking *chana dal* in 4 cups of water for 2 or 3 hours. At the end of this time thoroughly wash the *chana dal* under running water and drain. Bring 3 cups of water and the salt to a boil in a medium-size pot. When the water begins to boil, add the *chana dal*. Wait for the water to begin its second boil, then cover the pot and cook over a medium-to-low heat for 30 minutes. After this time, remove the cover and stir up the *dal*. To the open pot add the cayenne, turmeric, cumin, coriander and the tamarind pulp (skin and seeds removed) or the combination of lemon juice and sugar. Stir the ingredients in the pot well and leave the pot to simmer uncovered while you prepare the next step.

In a separate small pot or frying pan heat the vegetable oil over a low heat and add the mustard seeds and chopped garlic to it. When the oil gets hot, the mustard seeds will begin to pop. When they have ceased popping, add the oil mixture with seeds and garlic to the simmering pot of *dal*. Immediately cover the pot and keep covered for 2 minutes while the *dal* continues to cook over a medium-to-low flame. Then remove the cover and stir once with a spoon to mix in the new ingredients. Cook uncovered for another 5 minutes and the *dal* is ready to be served with rice or *parotha* (page 150) or both. Taste to correct seasoning i.e. salt. This *dal* is fairly thick in consistency and should not be made thinner with the addition of more water.

Serves Four to Six

MUNG DAL (DRY)

1 cup mung dal (without skin)
2-1/2 cups water
1 teaspoon salt
1 tablespoon vegetable oil
1/4 teaspoon black mustard seeds
1 clove garlic, chopped
1/4 teaspoon chopped fresh ginger
1/4 teaspoon garam masala*
1 small tomato, chopped

*see glossary

Mung beans are green when they are left whole. But when the *mung* beans are split in half and the green skins are removed, the resulting *mung dal* is yellow. You will also find *mung dal* that is green, where the skins have been left on. For this recipe the yellow, skinned *mung dal* is best.

This *dal* is one of the quickest cooking and easiest to make. Bring the 2-1/2 cups of water to a boil in a medium size pot and add the salt to it. After carefully sorting out the *mung dal* by hand, to remove any foreign objects, wash clean under running water and drain out the excess water. Add the washed and drained *mung dal* to the pot of boiling water. When the water begins its second boil, reduce heat to medium and cook uncovered for 10 minutes. Then, place a tightly fitting lid on the pot and reduce heat to low. Cook for 10 more minutes, by which time the *mung dal* will have become soft. There should be almost no water left in the *dal* after this period of cooking. If there is some water left, stir the *dal* continuously until the water has evaporated.

Remove the pot from the heat and transfer the *dal* to a large bowl. Rinse the pot out with water and dry. Now place the vegetable oil in the dry pot and heat over a medium temperature. Add the mustard seeds, chopped garlic and chopped ginger to the oil. The mustard seeds will begin to pop and spatter when the oil becomes hot. When they have all popped, add the cooked *dal* to the pot. Stir for 1 minute and then add the *garam masala* and the chopped-up tomato. Using a wooden spoon mix all the ingredients well. Continue to stir for 5 minutes until the *dal* is well heated. This *dal* should be served hot. If you are preparing other foods, reheat the *dal* before you serve. While most *dals* are thin and soup-like, this particular preparation of *mung dal* comes out somewhat dry and lumpy by comparison. For a thinner *mung dal*, use the recipe on page 127 for *masoor dal,* but substitute *mung dal.* *Serves Four*

Dals

URAD DAL WITH YOGURT

1/2 teaspoon garlic chutney (see page 51)
1 cup urad dal
5 cups water
1 cup plain yogurt
1/4 teaspoon turmeric powder
1 teaspoon salt
2 teaspoons lemon juice
fresh coriander leaves* (optional)

*see glossary

If you do not have access to a store selling foreign foodstuffs, then you will have to order this lentil from one of the sources listed in the back of this book. The *urad dal* (sometimes spelled *udud* or *ured*) is formed from a small, black *urad* bean which is first skinned and then split in half. The split *urad* bean has a dusty white color, and in India it is also ground into a flour and used to make several types of snacks.

Begin by making the garlic chutney according to the recipe in this book. Set aside 1/2 teaspoon of the garlic chutney and store the rest in the refrigerator for some future use.

Mix 1 cup of water with the plain yogurt and beat with a fork until the yogurt is smooth. To this add the turmeric powder and the 1/2 teaspoon of garlic chutney. Now beat the yogurt mixture again with a fork to make an evenly smooth liquid, and set the bowl aside for the moment.

In a medium-size pot, bring 4 cups of water and the salt to a boil. While you are waiting for the water to boil, clean the *urad dal* under running water and then drain. When the water starts to boil, add the drained *urad dal*. Bring the water and *dal* to another boil and cook uncovered for 10 minutes. Stir once, cover the pot and lower the heat to between low and medium. Cook the *dal* for 20 minutes till its grains are easily mashed when pressed between two fingers. Remove the covered pot from the heat and let stand for 10 minutes. Then add the yogurt mixture, stir once and return the pot to a low heat. Cook the *dal* over a low heat for 10 more minutes stirring frequently. By this time the yogurt will have combined with the *dal* to form a thick sauce-like mixture. Turn the heat off and stir in the fresh lemon juice. If you like, top this with some finely chopped fresh coriander leaves.

Serves Four to Six

MASOOR DAL

1 cup masoor dal (skinned)

5 cups water

1 teaspoon salt

1/4 teaspoon each turmeric powder,
  cayenne, cumin powder,
  fresh chopped ginger, coriander powder

2 tablespoons oil

1/4 teaspoon black mustard seeds

1 dried hot red chili pepper

2 teaspoons lemon juice

1 tablespoon fresh coriander* (optional)

*see glossary

This small flat, brown lentil when skinned and split in half becomes the bright, orange-colored *masoor dal*. It is one of the quickest of all the *dals* to prepare. It can be made, from start to finish in less than a half hour.

Wash the *masoor dal* in warm water and drain. Bring 4 cups of water, to which the salt has been added, to a boil. When the water begins to boil, add the cleaned and drained *dal*. After the water begins to boil a second time let the *dal* cook uncovered for 5 minutes. Then lower the heat to between medium and low and cover the pot. Now cook the *dal* for 15 to 20 minutes until it is quite soft. Then add 1 cup of water. Stir again and add the turmeric, cayenne, cumin, finely chopped ginger and coriander. Stir the *dal* well with a spoon to mix in all the spices. Now transfer the mixture to a large bowl, clean and dry the pot and return it to the stove.

Pour the oil into the pot and begin to heat over a low flame. Add the mustard seeds and the dried pepper (broken into pieces and seeds removed) to the oil. As the oil heats up, the mustard seeds will begin to pop and spatter. When they have stopped spattering, add the cooked *dal* back into the pot. This will cause a rather loud "chuuum" sound to be made. Don't worry, this is the sign of an authentic Indian cook. Cover the pot now and let the *dal* simmer for 2 minutes. Then turn the heat off and stir in the fresh lemon juice. This *dal* is now ready to be served. Top the *dal* with fresh coriander leaves if you like.

Serves Four to Six

Dals

PANCHA DAL (FIVE DALS)

1/4 cup each toor dal, chana dal,
   mung dal, urad dal, masoor dal
8 cups water
1-1/2 teaspoons salt
1/4 teaspoon each garam masala*,
   turmeric powder, fresh chopped ginger
1 tablespoon oil
1/4 teaspoon black mustard seeds
1/4 cup finely chopped onion
1/2 fresh lemon
1 tablespoon unsweetened shredded coconut

*see glossary

This is a colorful holiday dish that uses five different *dals,* cooked in one pot. The different *dals* are added to the pot at different times, depending on how long it takes each to be cooked.

Wash each *dal* separately and keep in separate bowls. The *toor dal* must be washed very thoroughly in hot water to remove the coat of oil that acts as a preservative. Drain the *dals* and set them aside.

In a large pot, bring the 8 cups of water and the salt to a rapid boil. Add the *toor dal* by itself to the boiling water and cover. Reduce the temperature to a medium-low flame and cook for 10 minutes. Then add the *chana dal.* Cover and cook both the dals for another 10 minutes. After the second cooking period, add the *mung dal.* Allow all three *dals* to cook covered for yet another 10 minutes. Now add the last two *dals* to the pot, the *urad dal* and the *masoor dal.* Stir all the *dals* together and cook covered for 15 minutes. Now uncover the pot, stir all again and add the *garam masala,* turmeric and chopped ginger to the *dal* and stir. When the spices are well mixed in with the *dals,* leave the pot simmering with the cover off while you prepare the last step.

In a separate small pot or frying pan, begin heating the oil over a low temperature. Add the mustard seeds and the finely chopped onions to the oil. When the onions turn a light brown, add the oil with mustard seeds and onions to the simmering pot of *dals.* Cover the pot for 2 minutes while the oil mixes with the cooked *dals.* Remove the top once again and squeeze in the lemon juice. Continue to let the *dal* simmer for 2 more minutes while you stir all the ingredients together. Turn the heat off and top with the shredded coconut before serving.

Serves Six to Eight

Lentil and Dal-Based Dishes

Dal-Based Dishes

SAMBHAR

[handwritten: 4/26/96 Excellent!]

6 cups water
2 teaspoons salt
1/2 cup toor dal *[handwritten: — 1 C red lentils]*
pinch baking soda
1 tablespoon tamarind pulp*
   or 2 teaspoons lemon juice and 1 teaspoon sugar
1 large tomato
1 cup eggplant, cut into small cubes
1 cup carrots, cut into small cubes
1 cup small cauliflower buds *[handwritten: + fresh ginger]*
5 teaspoons oil
1/4 cup finely chopped onion *[handwritten: + fresh cilantro]*
1/2 teaspoon each cumin powder,
   coriander powder, turmeric powder
2 tablespoons shredded coconut *[handwritten: about 2 quarts]*
1/2 teaspoon black mustard seeds
4 whole peppercorns
1 dry red chili pepper (seeds removed)
pinch of hing* (optional)

*see glossary

[handwritten: 11/83 Very good also used red & green pepper slightly spicy]

[handwritten: + jalapeno + ginger]

Sambhar is a typically South Indian dish in which vegetables and dal are cooked together to produce a spicy and delicious dish.

In a large pot bring the water and 1 teaspoon salt to a boil. While you are waiting for the water to boil, wash the toor dal very thoroughly with very hot water, to remove the oil coating which acts as a preservative but must be completely removed before cooking. When the toor dal is free of its oily coating, drain off any excess water and add to the boiling water along with a pinch of baking soda. Wait until the water begins a second boil then let the dal cook, uncovered for 5 minutes over a medium-to-high flame. Now reduce the heat to low and cook the dal, covered, for 35 to 40 minutes. At the end of this cooking time the dal should feel soft.

Begin preparing the vegetables and other ingredients while waiting for the dal to cook. If tamarind is available to you, prepare it by first removing the seeds and the hard outer shell. In a small bowl let 1 tablespoon of the tamarind pulp

[handwritten: — add lemon ju at end — cayenne pepper for more heat — Fresh ginger — jalapeno — fresh coriander]

The Hemlock Society

PO Box 101810
Denver CO 80250
(800) 247-7421
Fax: (303) 639-1224
www.hemlock.org
E-mail: hemlock@hemlock.org

...k in 2 tablespoons of hot water, and put aside. ...the tomato into medium-size chunks and start ...ting the other vegetables according to their des...tion in the list of ingredients.

...When the *dal* has finished cooking, remove from ...t and add the cut-up tomato and the tamarind ...water mixture (or lemon juice and sugar). ...en cover the pot and let it rest aside.

...n a large frying pan over a medium-to-low ...me, put only 3 teaspoons of the oil and the ...ely chopped onion. When the onions become ...t and transparent, add the diced vegetables and ...té for 2 minutes. Next add the cumin, cor...der, turmeric, 1 teaspoon salt and shredded ...conut to the frying pan and continue to sauté ...another 5 minutes. When all the spices are well ...xed in with the diced vegetables, add the entire ...ntents of the frying pan to the pot of *dal*. Stir ...e *dal* and vegetables once, cover the pot and ...ow to cook over a low heat while you prepare ...the next step.

In another frying pan or small pot heat 2 teaspoons of oil over a medium heat. Add the mustard seeds, peppercorns and the dried red chili pepper (which has been broken into 3 pieces) to the oil. As the oil gets hot, the mustard seeds will begin to pop. When they have finished popping and the chili pepper has turned a dark red, add the optional pinch of *hing*. Now add the complete contents of the frying pan to the pot of cooking *dal* and vegetables. Cover the pot immediately and cook for only 2 minutes. Then remove the lid and stir the ingredients once or twice.

Continue cooking all the ingredients in the uncovered pot for another 15 minutes over a low heat. After this time sample some of the vegetables to see if they are tender. If you feel that the vegetables are not thoroughly cooked, keep the pot simmering over a low heat for another 5 or 10 minutes. Serve the *sambhar* hot with rice and one of the breads described in the next chapter.

Serves Four

Dal-Based Dishes

DAL-DHOKALI (TOOR DAL WITH
CHICK-PEA FLOUR DUMPLINGS)

1 cup toor dal

10 cups water

1-1/2 teaspoons salt

1/4 teaspoon each turmeric powder, chopped
   fresh ginger, coriander powder, cumin powder

1 tablespoon tamarind pulp
   or 1 tablespoon lemon juice and 1 teaspoon sugar

1 large tomato, cut up

1 tablespoon oil

1/4 teaspoon black mustard seeds

4 whole cloves

1 dried hot red pepper

For Dhokalis (Dumplings)

1/4 cup besan (chick-pea flour)*

1/4 cup whole wheat flour

1 tablespoon oil

1/4 teaspoon salt

2 pinches cayenne

5 teaspoons water

*see glossary

The first step is to prepare the *dal*. Carefully wash the *toor dal* under very hot running water, rubbing the *dal* between the palms of your hands to remove all of the oily coating. This coating of oil acts as a preservative but must be completely removed before the *dal* is cooked. Drain the cleaned *dal* in a colander and set aside. In a large pot, bring the water and salt to a boil. When the water begins to boil, add the drained *toor dal* and continue cooking over a high flame until the water returns to a boil. Reduce heat to a moderate level and cook, uncovered, for 10 minutes. Stir the *dal* once and cover with a tight fitting lid. Cook the *dal* for 30 minutes and in the meantime, prepare the *dhokalis (doaklis)*.

Combine the whole wheat flour and the *besan* in a small bowl and mix with your hands until the two flours are well mixed together. Now add 1 tablespoon vegetable oil, the salt and cayenne to the bowl of flour. Crumble these ingredients together with the flour, using your fingers. Add 5 teaspoons of water to the bowl and begin to knead into a stiff dough with your fingers and palms as you would for a pie crust. If the flour is not moist enough to form a solid dough and instead crumbles as it is kneaded, add an additional teaspoon of water. This should make the dough moist enough to knead into a stiff ball. Put the ball of dough aside and check the pot of *dal.*

When the *dal* has cooked for 30 minutes, add the turmeric, chopped ginger, coriander, cumin and tamarind pulp (seeds and outer shell removed) or the mixture of lemon juice and sugar. Stir the *dal* once to mix in the spices and lower the heat. Let the pot of *dal* simmer for about 10 minutes, uncovered, while you finish preparing the *dhokalis.*

Moisten the palms of your hands with a little oil and begin kneading the ball of dough. Knead for a few minutes until the dough takes on a fairly smooth but still stiff consistency. Before you begin rolling out the dough, put a little oil on the rolling surface and on the rolling pin. Flatten the ball of dough with the palm of your hand and start rolling the dough from the center outwards. Roll it out flat until it is about the thickness of a plate. With a knife, cut the flattened dough into squares or diamonds about 1 inch by 1 inch. Add the squares of dough to the simmering *dal* a few at a time, making sure that they do not stick together. After you have added all the *dhokalis* to the *dal,* stir carefully to separate any of the *dhokalis* that might have stuck together. Now add the chopped-up tomato to the pot, stir once and simmer over a low temperature for 5 minutes or so, while you prepare the last step.

Place 1 tablespoon of oil in a small pot over a moderate flame, and add the mustard seeds, whole cloves and the dry red hot pepper (seeds removed and broken into 3 pieces) to the oil. As the oil heats up the mustard seeds will begin to pop. When they are no longer popping, add the entire contents of this pot to the larger pot of simmering *dal-dhokali.* Stir once to mix in the oil and mustard seeds. Now cook the pot of *dal-dhokali* covered, for 20 minutes, still over a low flame. Stir the contents of the pot every 5 minutes so that the *dhokalis* do not stick to the bottom of the pot. The *dhokalis,* as they cook, will become soft and swell to twice their original thickness. At the end of 20 minutes, taste the *dhokalis.* If they are soft and cooked all the way through, the dish is ready to be served. Serve the *dal-dhokali* hot with rice and make sure that everybody gets a few of the *dhokalis.*

Serves Eight

Dal-Based Dishes

PUNJABI CHANA

1 cup whole dried chana
   (chick-peas or garbanzo beans)
6 to 8 cups water
1-1/2 teaspoons salt
2 tablespoons ghee* or clarified butter
1/4 cup finely chopped onion
1 clove finely chopped garlic
1/2 teaspoon chopped fresh ginger
1/4 teaspoon each garam masala*, turmeric
   powder, cumin powder, coriander powder
1/4 teaspoon cayenne (optional)
1/2 fresh lemon

*see glossary

Chana, otherwise known as chick-peas or garbanzo beans, are available in a variety of ethnic neighborhood stores, as well as some supermarkets. There is a slight difference between the Spanish variety garbanzo bean and the Indian *chana* or Middle Eastern chick-pea. The garbanzo is a little larger and harder than the chick-pea or *chana.* If you have a choice, use the *chana* or chick-pea for cooking, although the garbanzo bean also will give excellent results.

Soak the *chana* in 3 cups of water for 10 to 12 hours or longer. I usually let them soak overnight, so that I must plan to make this dish one day in advance. When the *chana* is finished soaking, wash under running water and drain. Place 4 cups water and 1 teaspoon salt in a large pot over a high flame and bring to a boil. When the water begins to boil add the presoaked *chana.* Allow the water to come to a rapid boil once more. Then lower the heat to medium-low; cover the pot and cook the *chana* for 45 minutes. Now turn the heat off and drain the water that the *chana* was cooking in, into a bowl. Save this liquid as it will be used later on. Remove the cooked *chana* from the pot and set aside in another bowl.

Place the *ghee* or clarified butter in a large frying pan, over a low heat. Add the finely chopped onions, garlic and ginger and stir until the onions are lightly browned. Now add the well-drained *chana, garam masala,* turmeric, cumin, coriander and 1/2 teaspoon salt. For added hotness, also add the optional 1/4 teaspoon of cayenne. Sauté the mixture for 6 or 7 minutes so that all the spices are blended into the other ingredients. Now add 1-1/2 cups of the reserved *chana* water to the frying pan. Raise the heat to between medium and high and bring the liquid in the frying pan to a boil, but do not cover the pan. Let the liquid boil for 2 minutes then cover the pan and reduce the heat to low. Cook for 40 minutes till the beans are very soft but not mushy.

Almost all the liquid should be used up at the end of this cooking time; if the *chana* are not soft, however, and the water is gone, add 3 more tablespoons water and cook for another 5 to 10 minutes as needed. When the *chana* is finished cooking, remove the frying pan from the heat and squeeze the lemon juice over the top. Stir once, correct seasoning and serve with rice or another vegetable dish. This dish can also be served alone as a snack or with a little plain yogurt.
Serves Six

Dal-Based Dishes

DOODHI-CHANA-NU-SHAK

1/2 cup chana dal (split chick-peas)
1 pound doodhi* (opo or ghiya)
or 1 pound zucchini
3 tablespoons peanut oil
1/4 teaspoon black mustard seeds
1/4 teaspoon finely chopped fresh ginger
1 finely chopped garlic clove
1/4 teaspoon each cumin powder, turmeric
   powder, coriander powder, cayenne
1 teaspoon salt
1 tablespoon tamarind pulp*
or 2 teaspoons lemon juice plus 1 teaspoon sugar
1 tomato, cut up

*see glossary

The Philippine or Chinese *opo* is the equivalent of the Indian *doodhi* or *ghiya*. If this vegetable is unavailable to you, then substitute zucchini for the *doodhi* and you will end up with a similar-tasting dish. This is an excellent recipe in which a *dal* and a vegetable are cooked together.

First soak the *dal* in 2 cups of water for 2 hours. Then wash it under running water and drain. Scrape or peel the skin from the *opo* or the zucchini, and cut into approximately 1-inch squares. Set the cut-up vegetable and the drained *dal* aside in separate bowls.

In a medium-size pot, begin heating the oil over a moderate temperature. As the oil is heating, add the mustard seeds, chopped ginger and garlic. When the oil gets hot the mustard seeds will begin to spatter and pop. When the spattering has stopped, add the well-drained *chana dal* and sauté for 5 minutes. Now add the cut-up *opo* or zucchini, cumin, turmeric, coriander, cayenne and salt. Mix all the ingredients together for 2 minutes. After the ingredients are well mixed in, add 1 cup water to the pot and stir once. Add the tamarind pulp (seeds and shell removed) or the mixture of lemon juice and sugar. Cover the pot and cook over a moderate heat for 15 to 20 minutes. Check after 15 minutes to see if the vegetable is tender and the *dal* is soft but not falling apart. When the vegetable and *dal* are sufficiently cooked, turn off the heat. Add the cut-up tomato to the pot, stir once, cover and let stand for 2 or 3 minutes before serving.
Serves Four

Dal-Based Dishes

MUNG DAL WITH SPINACH

1 cup yellow mung dal (skinned) or masoor dal
2 bunches spinach (about 1 pound)
4 tablespoons vegetable oil
3 tablespoons finely chopped onion
3 finely chopped garlic cloves
few pinches whole cumin seeds (optional)
1/4 teaspoon cayenne
1 tablespoon fresh lemon juice
1 teaspoon salt

Here is another simple and quick way of cooking a vegetable together with a *dal*.

Soak the *mung dal* in 2 cups of water for 2 to 3 hours. Then wash the *dal* under running water, drain it completely and put it aside. Wash the spinach thoroughly so that all the dirt and sand is removed. Drain the spinach leaves and chop or tear them into fairly large pieces. (The spinach in India is smaller and the leaves do not have to be cut at all.)

In a medium-to-large-size frying pan, begin heating the oil over a moderate flame. Add the chopped onion, garlic and optional cumin seeds to the oil. As soon as the onions begin to brown, add the well-drained *mung dal* and sauté for 2 minutes. Now add the drained spinach pieces to the frying pan and sauté the spinach and *mung dal* for 10 minutes, stirring quite frequently. The spinach leaves will shrink and almost seem to shrivel down to nothing. Stir the *dal* and spinach often while sautéing so that none of the *dal* will stick to the bottom of the pan. After the 10 minutes, stir in the cayenne, lemon juice, salt and 4 tablespoons of water. Stir the ingredients in the frying pan once and lower the heat to the lowest possible setting. Cover the frying pan with a tightly fitting lid and cook for 10 more minutes. Do not cook for longer than this as the spinach will be reduced almost to the point of non-recognition.

This is considered a dry *dal* because there is no sauce-like quality to the finished dish. This dish should be served with rice and another vegetable that has a sauce.

Serves Four

Dal-Based Dishes

KHATA MUNG (SOUR MUNG)

1 cup yogurt or undiluted buttermilk
5 cups water
1/4 teaspoon turmeric powder
1/2 teaspoon garlic chutney (see page 51)
1 teaspoon salt
1 cup whole mung beans
2 pinches baking soda
1 tablespoon chopped fresh
   coriander leaves* (optional)

*see glossary

Mung beans are one of man's oldest food sources. When Buddhists from India journeyed to China to spread the teachings of Buddhism, they took *mung* beans with them so that they would have no trouble maintaining a vegetarian diet in a foreign land. Even after the influence of Buddhism diminished in China the *mung* sprout continued to play an important role in Chinese cuisine. Even to this day the nutritious and protein-rich *mung* bean and *mung* sprouts can be purchased in almost any store that sells Chinese food items. *Mung* beans are also a popular item among health food enthusiasts and can generally be purchased in health food stores.

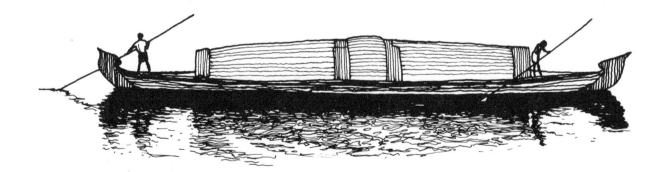

Dal-Based Dishes

Begin by mixing 1 cup of yogurt (or buttermilk) and 1 cup of water together with a fork until a uniformly thick liquid is formed. Stir the ground turmeric into the yogurt liquid and set the bowl aside.

Make the garlic chutney according to the recipe. You will get about 4 teaspoons of garlic chutney of which you will need only 1/2 teaspoon. The unused chutney can be stored in a refrigerator for two weeks until it is needed. Add the 1/2-teaspoon of garlic chutney to the bowl of yogurt and water and mix with a fork so that the chutney is well mixed into the liquid.

In a medium-size pot, bring 4 cups of water and the 1 teaspoon salt to a boil. While waiting for the water to boil, thoroughly wash the *mung* beans in cold water and drain. Now add the *mung* to the boiling water along with the baking soda, which speeds the cooking process. Allow the pot to cook uncovered over a high flame until the water begins to boil again. Now lower the heat to medium and continue to cook uncovered, for 10 minutes. Then reduce the heat to medium-low and cover the pot. Cook for 45 minutes or till the *mung* feels very soft when pressed between two fingers. You will notice that some of the *mung* beans have completely broken apart; this is as it should be. In India, some of the cooked *mung* is taken out at this point to be fed to the children. The *mung* is soft and easily digested but not yet hot with spices.

Remove the pot of cooked *mung* from the heat and let stand, still covered, for 15 minutes. Then add the prepared yogurt liquid. Stir all the ingredients together with a spoon and return the pot to the stove. Cook the *mung,* uncovered for another 1/2 hour over low heat, stirring frequently. After this time all the ingredients will have combined with the yogurt mixture and the *mung* to form a thick, rich sauce. Taste and correct the seasoning. The *khata mung* is now ready to be served over rice. For an added flavor, chopped coriander leaves (Chinese parsley) can be used as a topping.

This same dish can be prepared with unskinned (green) *mung dal* instead of whole *mung*. In this case it will only need 1/2 the cooking time of the whole *mung*.

Serves Four to Six

Dal-Based Dishes

SABAT MAAHN (WHOLE BLACK LENTILS)

1 cup whole urad*
10 cups water
1 teaspoon salt
large pinch baking soda
1/2 teaspoon turmeric powder
1/4 teaspoon garam masala*
1/2 teaspoon finely chopped fresh ginger
2 tablespoons butter or ghee*
1/4 cup finely chopped onion
2 cloves garlic
1 whole red, dried chili pepper

*see glossary

Whole *urad* is a small black lentil, also known as *maahn* beans in India. The whole *urad* should not be confused with the large black beans commonly sold in most grocery stores in the West. This particular preparation is from the state of Punjab, where it is considered an essential dish to be served during a wedding feast.

As with any imported lentil, first sort out any stones and other foreign objects. Pour 10 cups of water into a large pot and bring to a boil. While waiting for the water to boil, wash the *urad* beans in hot water to remove any dust on the beans and then drain. When the water begins to boil, add the beans, salt and baking soda. Bring the beans and water to another boil and continue boiling for 15 minutes, uncovered, over a moderate heat. Now lower the heat to a medium-low flame and cook the *urad*, covered, for another 45 minutes. Then add the turmeric, *garam masala* and chopped ginger. Mix the ingredients with a spoon, recover and cook for 30 more minutes. By this time the *urad* beans should all have broken apart to form a thick sauce with the water and spices. Let the *urad* simmer, uncovered, for 5 or 10 minutes while you prepare the last step.

In a small pot or frying pan, begin heating the butter or *ghee* over a very low heat. When the butter has melted, add the chopped onion and garlic. Break the dried pepper into 3 pieces and remove any seeds, then quickly add these pieces to the melted butter. When the onions become a light brown, add the contents of this pot (including the oil) to the larger pot of simmering *urad*. Mix with a spoon and let the dal simmer for 5 or 10 more minutes. Serve with rice and *parotha* (page 150).
Serves Six

Dal-Based Dishes

MOTH (MUTH)

1 cup moth (brown lentil)
4 cups water
3 tablespoons vegetable oil
3 cloves finely chopped garlic
pinch of hing* (optional)
1 teaspoon salt
1/4 teaspoon each turmeric powder,
   cayenne, coriander powder
1/2 fresh lemon

*see glossary

This small brown lentil is imported from India, and is available in stores selling Indian dry goods. *Moth* (sometimes spelled *muth* or *math*) has a unique flavor among all the lentils. When prepared according to this recipe, the *moth* becomes a thick almost dry dish that is served alongside rice rather than over the rice. *Moth* can be served as an afternoon snack, either by itself or with a little plain yogurt.

First sort out any foreign objects such as little stones from the grain. Then, soak the *moth* in 2 cups of warm (not hot) water for 6 hours, in a covered bowl. You will notice that after the lentils have soaked, they will have puffed up a bit and will be soft to the touch. After soaking, wash in warm water and drain.

In a medium pot or frying pan, begin heating the oil over a medium flame. Add the chopped garlic to the oil. When the pieces of garlic turn brown, add the optional pinch of *hing* and the well-drained *moth*. Sauté the *moth* for 5 minutes and then add the salt, turmeric, cayenne and coriander. Continually stir the ingredients in the pot or frying pan for 2 minutes, till all the spices have been well mixed in. Now add 2 cups of water to the pot and reduce the heat to low. Stir the ingredients once, cover with a tightly fitting lid, and cook for approximately 1 hour over a low heat. Check the pot after 30 minutes to see if there is sufficient water left for the last 1/2 hour. If not, add 2 or 3 tablespoons more water and recover. At the end of an hour's cooking time the *moth* should be tender and there should not be any water left in the pot. If some water is left, cook uncovered for a few minutes, stirring continuously so that all the water evaporates. When the *moth* is done, remove the pot from the heat and squeeze the lemon juice over the top, then mix once or twice. This lentil can be served hot, warm or cold.
Serves Six

Breads

Breads

Bread has been relegated to a position of minor importance in many areas of the West. It is often tasteless and nutrition-lacking and rarely is it made at home. In most of Asia, the statement that bread is the staff of life takes on a much fuller meaning. Throughout most of Asia the flat or unleavened bread is prepared and served with almost every meal. These breads prepared from unadulterated whole wheat flour are full of nutritional goodness and are incomparably delicious. I think one of the great joys of eating in an Indian home, is being served freshly cooked breads while you are eating. The woman of the household, who eats after the men and guests are finished, dutifully prepares these breads as you are eating so that the moment you have finished your last *chapati* or *parotha*, you will immediately be served a fresh and piping-hot bread before you have a chance to refuse it.

The texture of the raw flour is very important to the final quality of the cooked bread. In India the flour is ground into many different grades according to the type of bread that is being cooked. In the West, best results can be obtained from whole wheat *pastry* flour, available in many grain stores. If this grade of flour is not easily obtainable, then good results may also be gotten from a mixture of half regular whole wheat flour and half white, all-purpose flour.

The most important step in preparing the dough for any of the breads in this chapter is the kneading of the dough to the proper consistency. Once the dough has been evenly and thoroughly kneaded, the rolling out and cooking of the different breads will be simple. You will notice that in each recipe, the list of ingredients calls for the addition of "1/2 to 3/4 cup of water." This measure varies according to the amount of moisture in the air. You should always first add 1/2 cup water to the 2 cups flour and see if that is enough to bind the flour into the proper consistency. If not, then add the remaining 1/4 cup of water, 1 tablespoon at a time, until the desired consistency is achieved.

A girl grows up in India watching her mother make the different types of breads; the everyday varieties such as *chapatis* and *bhakharis* and the much-waited-for, special-occasion breads which are made on different holidays. This young girl acquires the techniques necessary to make perfect breads at a very early age. Now I think how simple and easy it is to mix the flour, knead the dough, roll out the breads and cook them to perfection at a moment's notice. But this seemingly casual attitude belies the many years of learning and practice that have made these techniques seem so easy and natural to me now. Do not be put off by this admission. Indian bread-making is easy and with a little patience and practice your efforts will be rewarded.

Breads

CHAPATIS

2 cups whole wheat pastry flour
or 1 cup regular whole wheat and 1 cup
   all-purpose flour
2 tablespoons vegetable oil
1/2 teaspoon salt (optional)
1/2 to 3/4 cup water
ghee* or clarified butter as needed

*see glossary

Chapatis are soft, thin, round, unleavened breads that appear very much like the Mexican corn tortillas and are the most commonly made bread in most of India. Many Indian women will prepare *chapatis* twice a day, and if any are left over they will be saved for the next day's morning tea. Although *chapatis* (pronounced cha-pa-teas) are common in India, it does not mean they are considered ordinary. In fact most Indians prefer this bread over any other bread, and as such, the *chapati* has become an almost inseparable part of any truly Indian meal. In different parts of India *chapatis* are called by different names such as *roti, rotli* and *phulka.*

I would like to make a comment here about the art of rolling a round *chapati.* Ideally a *chapati* should asume the shape of a perfect circle. This skill, that of being able to roll a perfect circle from a mound of dough, is one that is acquired from many years of practice. It makes little difference to the taste of the *chapati* if it is round or square. But a round *chapati* has a certain aesthetic quality that is deemed quite important by most Indians. I had traveled through many of the countries of the world to reach India, after having spent 5 years in the United States. Upon arriving home I was expected to once again help prepare the family meals. After a year of traveling, and 5 years of school, I was a little out of practice in the making of *chapatis.* Nevertheless I rolled out the *chapatis* as nearly round as I could. When I served them to my father, he looked at them and then casually asked me if I had, in fact, made maps from the *chapatis* of those countries that I had visited.

On the list of ingredients, salt is listed as an option because many people in India prefer their *chapatis* made without salt, although I personally prefer *chapatis* made with salt.

Read the introductory notes on flour and kneading dough before you begin. Start off by combining the flour, salt and oil in a large wooden or ceramic bowl. Use your fingers to rub the oil into the flour, until the oil is evenly distributed throughout the flour. When this is finished, add 1/2 cup of water to the bowl and begin kneading the flour and water with both hands so as to form a dough. If the flour and water do not combine fully and the flour begins to crumble, then more water is needed. Still kneading, add 1 tablespoon of water at a time until the dough holds together. You should not have to add more than 3 or 4 tablespoons of water at most. When the dough forms a single mass, remove from the bowl and transfer to a flat wooden surface that has been lightly greased with a few drops of oil. Continue to knead the dough, pushing it with the palms of your hands while continually folding the dough around itself. Knead the dough in this manner for 10 to 15 minutes until it takes on a stiff but smooth texture. The dough should have the consistency of stiff pizza dough when finished. Gather the dough into a ball.

In these next steps to finish the *chapatis,* you will need a rolling pin, a heavy iron frying pan and a towel. You will also need a little flour and *ghee*.

Now break the ball of dough into 12 equal pieces. First roll each piece into a ball and then press flat between the palms of your hands. The flattened pieces of dough should be approximately 2 inches in diameter; they are known as *gornas* in India. Next sprinkle a little flour on the rolling surface. In India we use a small, round table to roll the *chapatis* out on. This small table, called a *patli,* helps one to roll a more circular *chapati,* but any flat surface can be used. At this point, place the heavy pan over a medium heat so that the cooking surface will be sufficiently hot by the time the first *chapati* is rolled out.

Using the rolling pin, roll out the first piece of dough into a round disc about 6 inches in diameter. Try to make the *chapati* as round and evenly flat as possible. Place the single rolled-out *chapati* on a dry surface and then roll out two more *chapatis* in the same fashion. The *chapatis* are best rolled out in groups of 3, so that they do not dry out while waiting to be roasted.

Have a dish of *ghee* or clarified butter waiting near the frying pan so that it can be spread over the hot *chapatis*. Place the first of the 3 chapatis on the hot frying pan. Cook on one side for 30 seconds, turn over with a spatula, and cook the second side for 30 seconds. Then turn again. Now using a towel, press down lightly over the surface of the *chapati*. If the bread swells somewhat at this point, it is a good sign. If not, do not worry. Turn the *chapatis* over again and continue to cook and turn a few times until both sides are done.

Breads

A finished *chapati* should be freckled with brown spots on both sides. Or it may have just a single large brown spot on both sides, depending on whether the *chapati* swelled up while it was being cooked. The first *chapati* is sort of a sample that tests the hotness of the cooking surface and also acts to season the cooking surface. There are really no strict rules on how many times a *chapati* should be turned over or how long it should be cooked. You should cook it and turn it over as many times as it takes for both sides to be fully cooked without burning.

After the *chapati* is sufficiently cooked, remove from the frying pan and place in a clean dish. Quickly spread 1 teaspoon of *ghee* or butter over the top surface of the *chapati* and begin cooking the second one. Finish roasting all 3 *chapatis*, stack them one on top of another and spread *ghee* or clarified butter over the top surface. Cover them with a towel and lower the heat under the frying pan. Now roll out the next batch of 3 *chapatis* and cook in the same fashion. Continue this sequence of rolling out and cooking until all the *chapatis* have been cooked. These breads should be served immediately so they are hot when eaten. When cooking a whole dinner the *chapatis* should be made last so that they will be hot when served. In India, when many *chapatis* have to be made, the task is simplified by having one person roll out the *chapatis* while another person cooks them and spreads the *ghee* over them.

If it should be necessary to reheat the *chapatis*, heat each one separately in a hot frying pan rather than using the oven. Reheat each side for only a few seconds to keep the bread from drying out and becoming stiff.

Makes about Twelve Chapatis

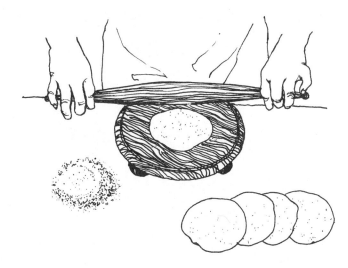

Breads

BHAKHARIS (GUJARATI STYLE)
1 cup whole wheat pastry flour
1/4 teaspoon salt (optional)
1 tablespoon vegetable oil
3 to 4 tablespoons water
ghee* or clarified butter as needed

*see glossary

Bhakharis (pronounced bak-ha-rees) are very much like thick *chapatis* described in the previous recipe. Since not as much care is required to roll out these breads, they are usually made either for breakfast or when a simple meal is called for.

Begin by combining the flour, salt and oil in a large bowl. Rub the flour between your fingers so that the oil is evenly distributed. Now add 2 tablespoons of water to the bowl and mix together using both of your hands. The flour will begin to bind together. Continue to knead the dough until it becomes a little stiff, then add another tablespoon of water and knead until the dough is smooth and not flaky. Add the fourth tablespoon of water only if it is necessary to make the dough smooth. Remove the dough from the bowl and place on a lightly greased rolling surface. Knead the dough for 10 to 15 minutes using the palms of your hands. The kneading process is the same as described for chapatis in the previous recipe.

When you have finished kneading the dough, gather it up into a ball and break it into 5 equal pieces. Take each piece and first roll into a ball and then flatten out between your palms. When all 5 pieces have been flattened out, take one and place on a lightly floured rolling surface. Using a rolling pin, roll out each flattened piece of dough into a circle about 4 to 5 inches in diameter. Try to roll the *bhakhari* out so that it is uniformly thick and as round as possible. It is not necessary to roll out this bread as thinly as the *chapatis* described in the last recipe. Rolling out *bhakharis* is a simple and quick process. Roll out all 5 *bhakharis* and set aside on a dry surface.

Place a heavy iron skillet over a moderately high flame and wait until the surface becomes hot. Reduce the heat to medium and place the first *bhakhari* in the pan. Cook on one side for 30 seconds, then turn over with a metal spatula and cook on the second side for 50 to 60 seconds. Turn the *bhakhari* over once again and with a kitchen towel, gently press down on the *bhakhari* at different spots; this helps it cook evenly. Sometimes the *bhakhari* will blow up like a balloon. If this happens, simply press down on the dough very gently, then wait a few seconds and turn it over. Cook another 15 seconds or so until both sides are covered with a number of brown spots, which indicates that the *bhakhari* is done. Spread a teaspoon of *ghee* or clarified butter over the top of each cooked *bhakhari*. Cook the remaining 4 *bhakharis* in the same manner, spreading *ghee* over the top and stacking one on top of the other. These breads should be served hot with a meal or with breakfast tea. If any are left over, they can be saved and eaten cold on the following morning.
Makes Five Bhakharis

Breads

PAROTHA (PLAIN)

2 cups whole wheat pastry flour
or 1 cup regular whole wheat and
   1 cup all-purpose flour
1/2 teaspoon salt (optional)
3 tablespoons vegetable oil
1/2 to 3/4 cup water
ghee* or clarified butter as needed

*see glossary

A *parotha* (pronounced pa-roe-ta) is actually two *chapatis* (page 144) rolled together to make a multi-layered bread which is then roasted with a layer of *ghee* spread on both sides. Even though the composition of the dough is quite similar to that of *chapatis,* the layering of the bread and the cooking with *ghee* make the *parotha* a unique bread.

To make the dough, add the flour, salt and oil to a large bowl. Using your fingers, rub the oil into the flour and mix the ingredients together. When the oil is evenly distributed throughout the flour, add 1/2 cup water and begin mixing together with both hands. The flour will begin to bind together to form a dough as you blend the mixture with your hands. Add more water a tablespoon at a time, while you continue to knead, until the dough is not flaky, but soft and smooth. You may not have to add the entire 1/4 cup water to the dough before it becomes smooth.

Remove the dough to a flat surface that has been lightly greased with a few drops of oil. Continue to knead the dough using the palms of your hands to push the dough out of shape, then wrap the dough around itself and begin the pushing motion again. Continue to knead the dough in this manner for a full 10 minutes. When the kneaded dough has achieved an evenly smooth texture, gather the dough into a ball and set aside.

For rolling out and cooking the *parothas* you will need a rolling pin, heavy metal skillet, some *ghee* or clarified butter and a little flour. Take the ball of dough and break into 20 equal-size pieces. Roll each piece into a ball and then flatten between the palms of your hands. Place the flattened-out pieces of dough on a dry surface. Sprinkle a little flour onto the rolling surface and the rolling pin. Take 2 of the flattened pieces of dough and roll out each into separate circles, approximately 4 inches in diameter. Place one of the rolled-out pieces of dough on top of the other one and using your thumb and index finger, pinch the edges together. Use enough pressure to seal the edges so that the dough merges together at the points where pressure is applied. Now sprinkle a little flour over the top of this layered piece of dough and very carefully roll it out into a larger circle approximately 7 inches in diameter. Be especially careful that the 2 circular pieces do not come apart while you are rolling out the larger *parotha*. After a *parotha* has been successfully rolled out,

set it aside on a dry surface. Roll out 2 more *parothas* by repeating the method just described.

Place the skillet over medium to high heat and allow the cooking surface to become hot. When the pan is hot, gently place one of the *parothas* on the cooking surface and cook for 1 minute before turning over. Cook the second side for 1 minute and turn over once again. Now spread 1 teaspoonful of *ghee* or clarified butter over the top surface of the *parotha* and turn over in the frying pan. Spread another teaspoonful of *ghee* or butter over the second side and remove from the pan if both sides are cooked. A finished *parotha* will be light brown in color with a number of dark brown spots covering both sides. Place the second *parotha* in the frying pan and repeat the cooking process. If the skillet becomes too hot and starts to smoke, reduce the heat to prevent burning.

Finish rolling out and cooking the *parothas* in groups of 2 or 3. Stack them on a dish, one on top of the other, and cover with a towel to keep them warm. *Parothas* should be served hot and are usually cooked in conjunction with other North Indian dishes.

Makes Ten Parothas

Breads

ALU PAROTHA
(POTATO FILLED PAROTHA)

Parotha

2 cups whole wheat pastry flour
or 1 cup regular whole wheat and
   1 cup all-purpose flour
1/2 teaspoon salt (optional)
2 tablespoons vegetable oil
1/2 to 3/4 cup water
ghee*or clarified butter for frying

Filling:

3 large potatoes (about 1 pound)
2 tablespoons oil
1/4 teaspoon cumin seeds
1/2 teaspoon salt
1/4 teaspoon turmeric powder
1/8 teaspoon cayenne

*see glossary

This is the Indian version of the potato pancake. Or if you are familiar with New York cuisine you would recognize the *alu parotha* as the counterpart of the venerable potato *knish.*

The first step is to prepare the potato filling. Wash the potatoes but leave on the skins. Place the potatoes in a pot with 6 cups of water, bring to a boil and boil until they are very soft so that the prongs of a fork readily pass through without sticking. Then remove them from the water, allow to cool and peel off the skins. Using a fork, mash the potatoes in a bowl to the consistency of a coarse mash. Do not use an electric blender or an egg beater for this as it will make the potatoes too smooth.

Add the 2 tablespoons oil to a medium-size saucepot and place over a low-to-medium temperature. After a minute, add the cumin seeds to the hot oil. When the cumin seeds darken after a minute or two, add the mashed potatoes, salt, turmeric and cayenne. Mix all the ingredients together with a wooden spoon for about 5 minutes. Remove the pot from the heat and set aside so that the potato mixture will cool down to room temperature while you are preparing the dough.

Prepare the dough in the exact same way as described in the previous recipe for plain parotha.

After it has been kneaded into a smooth consistency, divide it into 20 equal-sized pieces. Take each piece into your hands and first roll into a ball and then flatten between your palms. Finish flattening out all the pieces of dough and set them aside on a dry surface.

Sprinkle a little flour on a smooth surface. Take one of the flattened pieces of dough and roll it into a circle about 4 inches in diameter. Roll out a second piece of dough the same way. Try to roll out the dough so that the circles are as round and evenly flat as possible. Next, take a tablespoon of the potato mixture and spread it evenly over the surface of one of the circular pieces but leave 1/2 inch from the edge free. Cover the first piece with the second rolled-out piece of dough. Pinch the edges of the 2 circular pieces together by exerting a firm pressure with your thumb and forefinger around the edge.

Now gently roll out the *parotha* to approximately a 7-inch diameter circle. While rolling care must be taken so that none of the filling is allowed to slip out. Sprinkle a little flour over the dough as you are rolling it out, to prevent it from sticking to the rolling pin. Although it is not necessary, you may turn the *parotha* over while you are rolling it out. Prepare another potato-filled *parotha* in the same manner and cook them before rolling out the remaining dough.

Heat a large, heavy, iron frying pan over a medium temperature. When the pan is hot, carefully place one of the filled *parothas* on the cooking surface. Cook on one side for a minute, turn over with a metal spatula, cook on the second side for a minute and turn over once again. Spread 1 teaspoon of *ghee* or clarified butter over the top of the *parotha* and let it cook, without turning it, for another 1/2 minute. Now turn and spread a teaspoon of *ghee* or clarified butter over the second side and let cook for a minute. When both sides are lightly browned with a number of reddish brown spots, then the *alu parotha* is done. Stack the cooked *parothas* on a serving dish and cover with a towel to keep them warm. Continue to roll out the *parothas* and cook them in groups of two until they are all finished.

Alu parotha should be served warm with another vegetable dish or a *raita* or just with plain yogurt. When making this bread for an Indian meal, it is not necessary to prepare rice also. Although *alu parotha* takes both time and effort to prepare; it is a delight to eat.
Makes Ten Parothas

Breads

PURAN POLI
(PAROTHA STUFFED WITH DAL)

Parotha:
2 cups whole wheat pastry flour
or combine 1 cup regular whole wheat and
    1 cup all-purpose flour
2 tablespoons oil
ghee* or clarified butter for frying
1/2 teaspoon salt
1/2 to 3/4 cup water

Filling:
1/2 cup toor dal*
pinch of baking soda
6 whole cardamom pods
1/3 cup brown sugar

*see glossary

Puran poli is a variety of stuffed bread that is made in Gujarat. This bread has a slightly sweet filling and is either prepared when there are guests or made for some special occasion.

To prepare the filling, place 2 cups of water in a medium-size pot and bring to a boil. While waiting for the water to boil, wash the *dal* thoroughly under hot water. This *dal* may be coated with an oil, which acts as a preservative and must be thoroughly cleaned off before using. Drain the *dal* and add to the boiling water. Add the baking soda and cook, uncovered, over a medium heat for 10 minutes. After 10 minutes, cover the pot and cook for another 20 minutes over a low-to-medium heat.

While waiting for the *dal* to cook, prepare the cardamom pods. Break open the pods and remove the tiny black seeds that are contained within. Gather all the seeds together and using a rolling pin, grind them into a coarse meal.

Check the *dal* at the end of 20 minutes. It should be sufficiently soft so that when a grain is pressed between two fingers it will fall apart. If the *dal* is still hard, allow it to cook another 5 minutes and drain off any excess water. Now place the cooked *dal* over a low heat and add the sugar and ground cardamom seeds. Mix these ingredients together with a wooden spoon for 5 minutes or till the sugar has all dissolved. The filling is now ready;

remove from the stove and set aside, uncovered, so that it can cool to room temperature.

Prepare the dough for the *parothas* in exactly the same manner as described for plain *parothas* on page 150. Divide the dough into 20 equal pieces, each piece into a ball and then flatten with the palms of your hands. Now follow the directions for rolling out and filling the breads as described in the previous recipe for *alu parotha*. Simply substitute a tablespoon of the *dal* for the tablespoon of potato in each *parotha* and everything else is the same. After you have filled the *puran poli* with *dal*, roll out in the exact same manner as the *alu parotha*, being very careful that none of the filling escapes. The rolled-out *puran poli* can be quite thick and still cook properly.

Heat a heavy iron skillet over a medium temperature and place the first of the *puran polis* carefully on the cooking surface. Cook in exactly the same way as the *alu parotha*. When both sides are light brown and covered with reddish brown spots the *puran poli* is ready. Serve these breads hot with an extra spicy chutney, a vegetable dish, yogurt and rice. Some people will spread another teaspoon of *ghee* or melted butter over the *puran poli* just before serving.

Makes Ten Polis

Breads

PURIS (PUFFED BREADS)
1 cup whole wheat pastry flour
or 1/2 cup regular whole wheat and
  1/2 cup all-purpose flour
1/4 teaspoon salt (optional)
1 tablespoon vegetable oil
1/4 cup water
vegetable oil for deep frying

A delicate, light bread that is made for holidays and other special occasions. The dough is similar to that of other breads already described in this chapter. The difference is that the *puris* are deep fried in oil where they inflate like a balloon to form a puffed, thin-skinned bread that is a delight to eat.

In a large mixing bowl combine the flour, salt and vegetable oil. Mix these ingredients together by rubbing the oil into the flour with your fingers. Now add 1/4 cup of water to the bowl and begin blending the ingredients with both hands. Soon the flour and water will begin to bind together into a smooth, fine-textured dough. If the dough seems too dry and flaky, add another teaspoon of water while continuing to knead. Add still another teaspoon of water until the desired consistency is reached. Grease the surface of a rolling board with a few drops of oil and transfer the dough from the bowl to the greased surface. Continue to knead the dough by pushing it back and forth with the palms of your hands while wrapping the dough around itself. Knead the dough for 10 to 12 minutes until it takes on a very smooth consistency. Gather the dough into a ball and divide into 12 to 14 equal-size portions. Roll each piece into a ball and flatten between the palms of your hands.

Now place a few drops of oil on the rolling surface. With a light, even rolling motion, roll out each piece of dough into a 4-inch diameter circle. The roundness of the *puri* will affect how well the dough will inflate when cooked. Roll out all the *puris* and spread them out on a dry surface.

Pour 1-1/2 to 2 cups of vegetable oil in a shallow pot or a wok (the wok requires less oil than a pot). Heat over a medium flame until a piece of dough immediately bubbles to the surface when dropped in. When the oil is hot, take one of the round *puris* and gently ease it into the oil. The *puri* will first drop to the bottom and then rise to the surface. As soon as it reaches the surface, gently turn it over with a slotted or mesh spoon. If everything is right, the *puri* will now inflate like a balloon and float on the surface of the oil. Turn the *puri* again and cook until both sides are a light, golden brown. Do not be disappointed if the *puris* do not inflate every time. This might happen for any number of reasons, but the flat *puris* still taste very good. When the *puri* has finished cooking, remove from the oil and let the excess oil drain back into the wok or pot. Carefully place the *puris* in a serving dish lined with paper towels to absorb any oil still on them.

These delicious *puris* are usually served with some sweet dish such as *shrikhand* (page 63) or *kheer* (page 117). Or they can be served with plain yogurt, a vegetable dish, rice and a *dal,* for an Indian meal with a little special touch.
Makes Twelve Puris

MASALA PURIS (SPICY PURIS)

the same ingredients as listed in
the previous recipe for puris, plus

1/4 teaspoon cayenne
1/4 teaspoon turmeric powder
1/4 teaspoon cumin powder
or whole cumin seeds

Mix the flour, 1 teaspoon oil, salt, cayenne, cumin and turmeric together in a large mixing bowl. Rub the oil into the flour by rubbing the flour between your fingers. Now follow the previous recipe exactly. Add the necessary water, knead the dough, roll out and deep fry the *masala puris* as directed in the last recipe for plain *puris*.

These spicy, puffed breads go particularly well with a sweet dish such as *kheer* (page 117).

Makes Twelve Puris

MITHI PURIS (SWEET PURIS)

1 cup whole wheat pastry flour
or combine 1/2 cup regular whole wheat
   flour and 1/2 cup all-purpose flour
1 tablespoon vegetable oil
2 tablespoons brown sugar or honey
oil for deep frying

In India, sweet *puris* are very popular among children. On holidays when spicy, *masala puris* are made for the adults, sweet *puris* are made for the children.

Sweet *puris* are made the same way as plain *puris* (page 156). Simply add the sugar or honey with the flour and oil in the first step. If brown sugar is used, add 1/4 cup water; if honey is used, add 2 tablespoons water and bind the ingredients together to form a smooth dough. Then follow the procedure for kneading the dough and rolling out the *puris* as described in the recipe for plain *puris*. Deep fry as directed, except that the sweet *puris* should be allowed to become a little darker than the plain *puris*.

Makes Twelve Puris

Breads

PUDLA (BESAN PANCAKES)
1 cup besan* (chick-pea flour)
1 teaspoon whole cumin seeds
1 teaspoon salt
few pinches cayenne
1/2 cup water
1/2 cup finely minced onion
1/4 teaspoon finely chopped fresh ginger
1/2 cup diced tomato
oil for frying

*see glossary

This spicy, pancake-like snack is sometimes referred to as a vegetarian omelette. While more a snack or brief meal than a bread, it is included in this chapter because the main ingredient is flour.

In a large bowl, mix together the *besan,* cumin seeds, salt and cayenne (the amount of cayenne will directly affect how spicy the *pudla* is).

Then mix the water into the flour with your hands, breaking up any lumps with your fingers. Mix the ingredients until a smooth batter forms. Then add the finely chopped onion, tomato and ginger and stir with a spoon. The batter should now have a consistency that is a little thicker than pancake batter. If the batter is very thin, add a bit more flour and mix again.

Add 1 tablespoon of oil to a heavy iron frying pan and place over a moderate-to-high heat. When the oil is hot, place 2 tablespoons of batter in the center of the skillet and quickly spread the batter with the bottom of a spoon using a gradually widening circular motion. The batter should be spread to form a pancake approximately 4 inches in diameter. The circle need not be perfectly round, but it should be uniformly thick. Fry the *pudla* for 1 minute. Then carefully turn it over with a metal spatula and spread a teaspoon of oil over the cooked side. Let the second side cook for 2 minutes or so until it turns a light brown with a number of dark spots. Turn again if necessary so that both sides are sufficiently cooked. The brown and black spots do not mean that the *pudla* is burning, but rather that the *pudla* is satisfactorily cooked.

Serve the *pudla* hot with a helping of plain yogurt or with a vegetable or fruit salad.
Makes Six Pancakes

PAPADAM or PAPAD

If you have eaten in an Indian home or Indian restaurant you may be familiar with the crisp, potato-chip-like *papad,* or *papadam* as they are known in South India. The thin, brittle *papad* is served with a meal as a side item, in much the same manner as a chutney. No Indian feast would be complete without a *papad* and almost every important meal in India is accompanied by one of the hot varieties of *papad.*

The basic preparation of *papad* is very lengthy and complicated, requiring some 15 different ingredients and up to 10 days to prepare. Because the preparation is so elaborate most Indian homes and restaurants buy the uncooked, packaged variety of *papad.* These packages of dry *papad* can be bought from the Indian dry-goods stores listed in the back of this book.

Among the different varieties of *papad* are those made from *urad* flour, which are highly spiced, and the milder versions made from rice flour. The pack-aged dry *papad* available in the West come about 100 to a package and can last a number of months without refrigeration. These cannot be eaten straight from the package but must be first fried to give them their characteristic crispness. Prepare the *papads* using one of the following two methods.

Heat a heavy iron skillet over a medium flame. Place the *papad* in the frying pan and turn it over back and forth, very frequently, for about a minute or 2, until it turns a crisp, yellow-red. The *papad* is now ready to be served.

The second method involves deep frying the packaged *papad.* Heat 1 cup of oil in a wok or shallow saucepot. Ease the *papad* into the hot oil and deep fry for about a minute, until it turns red. Turn the *papad* over once or twice while waiting for it to change color. This second method produces a cooked *papad* that is a little more crisp than the first method.

Serve one *papad* to each person with his meal. Sometimes *papads* are served with tea as a snack.

Sweets

Sweets play a significant role in the multitude of holidays and feasts that are so much a part of India's rich culture. Sweets represent everything that is joyful; they symbolize prosperity and good fortune. The delightful quality of sweets and the degree to which they are savored and enjoyed, give them a place of importance somewhat greater than just the after-dinner dessert. When a special meal is prepared for a guest or for a holiday the meal will usually include one sweet-tasting item, since the distinct taste of the sweet, as opposed to a sour or spice flavor, is considered essential for a flavor-balanced meal. This sweet is served with the vegetable dish, rice and whatever else is prepared and is eaten during, rather than after, the meal. It is probably the costliness of the rich ingredients such as *ghee* and milk and the elaborate preparations of some of the sweets that have caused sweets to be so highly regarded by the people of India.

The sugar that is used in making most Indian sweets is a raw, unbleached variety of cane sugar. This sugar, known as *gur,* is actually healthier than the bleached and refined varieties available in the West. In some recipes I have substituted honey for sugar in an attempt to retain the nutritional goodness of the original preparations. For those sweets where substitution of honey was not feasible, I have used brown sugar instead. Although brown sugar in America is really only refined sugar and molasses mixed together, the taste is closer to the type of sugar that is used in India.

Sweets can be divided into two categories, those usually prepared at home and those that are purchased from "professional" sweet makers. In the first category are such things as *kheer* (a type of rice pudding), which have more of a loose or liquid consistency. The sweets in the second category are usually solid in texture and are purchased from *mithai-walas,* professional sweet makers. These *mithai-walas* are an institution in their own right in India. Each city or town will usually have a special section of the market where the sweet makers can be seen slowly mixing great bowls of milk and cream, carefully reproducing their age-old recipes for the different sweets. Each *mithai* or sweet shop is decorated by the very sweets that are being offered for sale. I can easily recall some of the tempting aromas that would arise from this colorful and popular section of my town. These sweet-makers are usually kept busy by the Indian ladies who are buying sweets for their children or for special occasions. But this part of the bazaar or market becomes really hectic when the religious holidays come around. During these times most Indian families purchase large quantities of prepared sweets to offer at the many feasts and celebrations.

This is not to say that there aren't many devoted cooks throughout India who are willing to spend the long hours necessary to make these special holiday sweets. Also some orthodox Hindu families who adhere to strict dietary practices will not entrust the preparation of any food they eat to someone who is not of their caste or family. The

Sweets

sweets that I have included in this chapter are those that are relatively easy to make and are usually made in the home by most Indians.

Many of the sweets described are prepared for the different important holidays. During these times, women will stock up on the different costly items that are necessary for the sweets. Then many days of preparation will begin. Houses will fill with delectable aromas and the children will squeal with delight and anticipation. Many times these sweets must be hidden from the children, lest the temptation be too great. The adults also are enlivened with the spirit of the festive occasions. It seems to me that when people work hard for their daily living, their times of celebration are more sincerely filled with joy and happiness.

In India most homes turn to the preparation of sweets during the last several weeks of the Hindu calendar year. These weeks in October or November are filled with many holidays, one right after another. In the Western State of Gujarat, where my home is, these weeks of holidays begin with *Shraddha*, a holiday in the memory of those who have died. At this time a particular day is chosen by each family on which a certain member of the family who has died will be remembered. On that day, the sweet that was most loved by the person being honored is prepared. When the dinner is ready on that day, the youngest member of the family takes a helping of the prepared sweet, folds it within a *chapati* (Indian bread) and places it on the roof of the house. Soon some birds gather and eat the sweet; it is said that at this time of the year

the souls of our ancestors reside in these birds. When the sweet has been eaten by the birds, it is a signal that the soul of the person who is being honored has been satisfied and that the feast can begin.

Following the holiday for dead souls is the holiday known as *Dashera*, which means "ten days." On these festive days the victory of Lord Rama over the evil Ravana is celebrated. This colorful and important story comes from the great Hindu epic, the *Ramayana,* and symbolizes for the people the triumph of the good over evil. Rama, the hero of *Ramayana,* was the ninth incarnation of Lord Vishnu who sustains the world. Prince Rama was chosen as heir to his father's throne when he reached adolescence; however due to some family quarrel he was exiled in the jungle for fourteen years. When he was staying peacefully in the jungle with his beloved wife, Sita, the wicked demon Ravana came, dressed up to look like a *sadhu* (holy man) and kidnapped the beautiful Sita to his kingdom Lanka. Rama sent his friend Hanuman, the Monkey God, to talk with Ravana about Sita's return. But the arrogant Ravana replied that the brave Rama must come with his army to release his wife. Hanuman trained a strong army of monkeys and Rama declared a war against Ravana. With Hanuman's army Rama fought the battle for ten days and became victorious on the tenth day.

These ten days are celebrated with much music and dancing and a different sweet is made for each of the days. As the evening approaches, the people gather in the streets dressed in their finest holiday clothes. The women look especially resplendent in their beautiful silk *saris*. Many of the men have flutes or *tablas* and soon the night is filled with glorious folk music and spirited dancing that lasts late into the evening. The tenth evening is considered the most important. On this night, huge paper and wooden statues of the good Lord Rama and the evil Ravana are erected in the center of the town. The hollow replica of Ravana is filled with firecrackers. When all the people of the town have gathered around these statues, a single flaming arrow is shot towards Ravana. As soon as the arrow touches Ravana, it sets off a most wonderful display that fills the sky with startling sounds and colors. The evil Ravana is vanquished and the audience applauds and shouts, as if the real battle and victory had just taken place. The children start the dancing, the men play their instruments and the ladies sing songs of Lord Rama and his beautiful Queen Sita. The evening finally ends with a great feast, at which time a variety of sweets is offered.

Soon after the ten days of *Dashera*, the biggest festival of the year begins. This is the festival of lights, known as *Divali*, which is celebrated all over India. The *Divali* festival lasts for 4 or 5 days on the last days of the Hindu calendar. Each day's festivities mark a different significant event which took place during the golden age of Lord Rama's rule over India. The preparations for this holiday begin weeks in advance. Many sweets must be made, new clothes are sewn for the children and the household begins a colorful transformation. Walls are painted and floors are decorated with intricate designs which are formed from multicolored chalk powders. During the evenings of *Divali*, all the houses are illuminated with countless candles and oil lamps. The sky is made bright by the colorful fireworks displays which each household sets off. Now is the time for the all-important sweets that have been bought or prepared many days in advance. Families and friends will visit each other during *Divali*, exchanging presents and eating the delicious sweets. The last evening of this holiday is celebrated by offering sweets to the Goddess Laxmi, in the hope that the following year will be fruitful for all. The next day is the Hindu New Year's Day and breakfast is prepared with at least one sweet so that the new year will start with sweetness. Hindu people gather at their temples to exchange New Year's good wishes and many sweets are distributed during elaborate ceremonies. At the end of New Year's Day the people return to their homes tired and hungry. With their dinner that evening they eat all the remaining sweets so that every dinner of the new year will be sweet.

Sweets

FIRNI (CREAM OF RICE PUDDING)

1/2 cup mixture almonds and
   pistachios (shelled and unsalted)
2 quarts milk
6 tablespoons cream of rice cereal (uncooked)
3/4 cup white sugar
1/2 teaspoon rose water
2 tablespoons butter

Prepare the shelled and unsalted nuts in the following manner. Soak the almonds in a cup of water for 1/2 hour, to loosen the outer brown skin of the almond; scrape off this outer skin with your fingernail, leaving the white almond beneath. Chop the almonds and pistachio nuts into small-to-medium-size pieces with the aid of a knife. Combine the nuts in a cup or bowl and set aside.

Pour the milk into a large, thick-walled pot and place over a high heat. As soon as the milk boils, reduce the heat to medium-low and, with a steady continous motion, stir the milk for 1/2 hour with a wooden spoon. Now slowly add the cream of rice to the pot of milk without interrupting your constant stirring motion. As you add the cream of rice, stir the milk with increased vigor to prevent lumps forming. After all the cream of rice has been added, begin adding the sugar while continually stirring the milk mixture. After all the sugar has been added, continue stirring for another 15 to 20 minutes, or until the mixture takes on a thick consistency, somewhat like pancake batter. Then remove the pot from the heat and let stand until the *firni* is warm but not hot. Now add the rose water and stir once. Pour the *firni* pudding into a large serving bowl or into individual dessert dishes.

Melt the butter in a small frying pan over a very low temperature. When completely melted, add the chopped almonds and pistachios and sauté them in butter for 5 minutes; remove the nuts with a slotted spoon and allow the butter to drain off. Gently pat the nuts dry with a paper towel to remove any excess butter. Now sprinkle the chopped nuts over the top of the *firni* in a decorative manner.

Chill the *firni* in the refrigerator for about 1/2 hour before serving. *Firni* can be served as a main course with *puris* (page 156) or at the end of any kind of meal as a dessert.
Serves Eight

SEV-BIRANJA (SWEET NOODLES)

2 quarts water

1 teaspoon salt

8 ounces sev (Indian wheat noodle also known as vermicelli) or 8 ounces thin spaghetti

1/4 cup melted butter or ghee*

1 cup dark brown sugar

1/4 teaspoon ground nutmeg or cinnamon

*see glossary

The thin wheat noodle known as *sev,* is prepared in the home in India, where it is sun dried and stored for many months. These noodles can be purchased or ordered from the stores specializing in Indian food products listed in the back of this book. The use of Italian-style thin spaghetti as a substitute for *sev* offers very good results. Sweet noodles are traditionally a Muslim dish in India, where they are prepared in a number of different ways. Here is one method of preparing this quickly made sweet.

In a large pot, bring the water to a boil; add the salt and stir. Break the *sev* or spaghetti into smaller pieces and add it to the boiling water. Boil the noodles, uncovered, for 10 to 12 minutes, until they are tender but not too soft. Stir a few times while they are cooking, so that they do not stick together. When the noodles have finished cooking, drain them in a colander and rinse with cold water. Shake the colander so that any excess water is removed.

In a heavy frying pan, heat the melted butter or *ghee* over a low flame for about a minute. Now add the well-drained noodles and sauté them, stirring with a wooden spoon for 5 minutes. Stir 3/4 of the cup of brown sugar into the noodles and continue stirring for 4 or 5 minutes until the sugar is well blended. Empty the noodles into two large, oven-proof pie plates (glass or metal) and spread out as thinly as possible. Sprinkle the remaining 1/4 cup sugar and the ground nutmeg or cinnamon over the top of the noodles. Put the pie plates under the broiler and cook for about 10 to 15 minutes until the top of the noodles becomes crisp and lightly brown. Do not overcook the noodles so that they all become hard.

You can serve *sev-biranja* with dinner, in place of rice or a bread. This sweet tastes best when hot but can also be eaten cold.
Serves Four to Six

Sweets

SHEERA (SIMPLE HALVA)

6 cardamom pods
3/4 cup melted butter or ghee*
2 cups water
3/4 cup honey or dark brown sugar
1 cup cream of wheat
or farina or cream of rice cereal (uncooked)
2 tablespoons chopped cashews
or chopped almonds
1/4 cup raisins

*see glossary

Sheera is one of the quickest and easiest of the Indian sweets to prepare. In India, *sheera* would be made for special guests, such as the parents of a prospective marriage partner. *Sheera* is also prepared for different religious occasions such as a wedding or a particular temple service, where the *sheera* is first offered to God, and then distributed among the participants of the ceremony as a *prasad* (God's leftovers). Children especially love these ceremonies that close with the distribution of the delicious *prasad*.

Begin by breaking open the cardamom pods and gathering the small seeds inside. Discard the outer shells, crush the seeds with a rolling pin and set aside.

In a saucepot, combine the water and honey or sugar and place over a low flame. Heat this mixture for 5 minutes, stirring occasionally till a syrup forms. The syrup should be hot but not so hot that the liquid boils. Turn the heat off and leave the pot of syrup on the stove until needed.

In a large, heavy frying pan, heat 1/2 cup of the melted butter or *ghee* over a low flame for 2 minutes. Be careful not to burn the butter. Gradually stir in the cream of wheat and regulate the temperature to between low and medium. Sauté the cream of wheat for 5 minutes, stirring it with a wooden spoon, then add the chopped nuts and continue to stir the mixture for another 5 to 7 minutes, till the cream of wheat turns a reddish color. Now add the previously made syrup to the cream of wheat and stand back a moment. The addition of the syrup will cause an immediate spattering which will last a few seconds, so be careful that you don't get burned. When the spattering stops, add the raisins and begin stirring the mixture again.

Stir the *sheera* with a constant, steady motion for 4 or 5 minutes. This will cause some of the liquid to evaporate and the *sheera* will start to draw away from the sides of the pan. As soon as it takes on a soft, lumpy consistency, empty it onto a clean serving dish. Add the ground cardamom seeds and the reamining 1/4 cup melted butter or *ghee*, over the top of the *sheera*. Often the *sheera* is served just at this point, by dishing out a handful of the warm sweet into the hand of the person being served. When offered as a *prasad*, it is most often served in this fashion. If you want the *sheera* to become solid so that it can be cut into pieces for serving, spread it out over the surface of the serving dish and put it in the refrigerator for 1/2 hour. Then remove and cut into slices or squares and serve.

Sheera is light enough to be served as a snack or as a side dish to a meal, replacing rice or bread. Or you can serve it with a western-style meal as a dessert.

Serves Six

Sweets

CARROT HALVA (WITH HONEY)

1/4 teaspoon crushed cardamom
1/4 cup shelled almonds
1/2 cup grated carrots
1 quart milk
1/2 cup honey
2 tablespoons melted butter

Begin by breaking open 8 to 10 whole cardamom pods and gathering the seeds together. Using a rolling pin or mortar and pestle, crush the seeds very finely and collect 1/4 teaspoon of the crushed seeds. Soak the shelled almonds in a cup of water for 1/2 hour to loosen the brown outer skin. Then remove the skins by scraping them off with your fingernail until the almonds are white.

Wash the carrots (2 should be enough) and scrape off the outer skin. Grate the carrots using the large or medium-size holes of a metal cheese grater. Do not try to use an electric blender for this as it will grate the carrots too finely.

Using a large wok or medium-size, heavy pot, bring the milk to a boil, stirring occasionally with a wooden spoon so that none of the milk sticks to the bottom. When the milk boils, add 1/2 cup of the grated carrots and reduce the heat to low. Cook the milk and carrots over a low heat for 45 minutes or longer, until the mixture is very thick. If you neglect to stir the mixture for even a moment, the ingredients will begin to stick to the bottom. At the end of the cooking time, turn off the heat.

Using an electric blender, chop the almonds into a coarse meal. If a blender is not available, first chop the almonds into small pieces with a knife and then grind them with a mortar and pestle.

Add the coarse almond meal to the pot containing the carrot and milk mixture and turn the heat on to low. Stir this mixture for 5 minutes and then add the honey, stirring until it is well blended into the other ingredients. Now add the melted butter and crushed cardamom seeds and stir all the ingredients for a minute or two. The *halva* should now be fairly thick and will form a single mass in the pot.

Empty the *halva* into a large dish or serving plate that has been lightly greased with a little melted butter. Using the flat part of your hand, spread the *halva* out until it forms a circle, leaving the last inch or 2 of the dish clear. Allow the halva to cool off for about 10 minutes until it is cool enough to touch. Then press down lightly with your hands and pat down the top surface. This patting down will serve to smooth out the top of the *halva* and to compact it slightly. Now place the *halva* in the refrigerator for about 40 minutes. At the end of this time, remove the dish and cut the *halva* into squares or pie-shaped slices. Serve with the meal or after, as a dessert.

Serves Six

DATE HALVA (WITH HONEY)

2 cups dates, seeds removed
1 cup shelled almonds
6 whole cardamom pods
4 tablespoons ghee* or clarified butter
2 tablespoons honey

*see glossary

Cut the dates into many small pieces and soak them in 1/2 cup water for 25 minutes. In an electric blender, grind the dates and water until they form a pulp-like consistency. Remove the date pulp and set aside. Chop the shelled almonds to the consistency of a coarse meal. This can be conveniently done with an electric blender or by simply chopping them with a knife and then grinding them under a rolling pin. Now open each of the cardamom pods and remove all the small seeds that are found within. Crush these seeds under a rolling pin as finely as you can.

In a medium-size frying pan, begin heating 2 tablespoons of the *ghee* or clarified butter over a very low flame. When the *ghee* is hot, add the ground almonds to the pan and sauté for a few minutes, making sure that the *ghee* or butter does not burn. When the almond pieces turn a reddish color, remove them from the frying pan and set them aside. Then add the remaining 2 tablespoons of *ghee* to the frying pan and heat over a very low flame. After a minute or so when the *ghee* becomes hot, add the honey and begin stirring with a continuous motion. The honey will combine with the *ghee* to form a syrup-like mixture. When the syrup starts to bubble, add the date pulp and continue to stir for 10 minutes, so that the date pulp completely blends with the honey and *ghee*. Now stir in the sautéed almond pieces and mix all the ingredients together. Add the crushed cardamom seeds and thoroughly stir them into the date mixture. Then turn off the heat.

Lightly coat a small dish or plate with a little *ghee* and empty the contents of the frying pan into it. After the *halva* has cooled down enough so that it can be handled, pat it down with the palm of your hand so that it covers most of the surface of the plate. Make the *halva* uniformly flat and as nearly round as possible. Cool the *halva* in a refrigerator for about an hour till it becomes firm enough to cut. Cut into thin pieces or small cubes and serve anytime.

Serves Four to Six

Sweets

LADOOS (SWEET BALLS)

1 cup whole wheat flour
1/2 cup cream of wheat cereal (uncooked)
3/4 cup ghee* or clarified butter
4 tablespoons water
1 cup melted ghee* or clarified butter
or Crisco for deep frying
6 cardamom pods
3/4 cup brown sugar
1 teaspoon khuskhus seeds (optional)*

* see glossary

One of the favorite gods of Hindu ladies is Ganesh, the Elephant God. Ganesh is admired by the ladies of India because he is a great admirer of good food. In fact the Elephant God's favorite food are the *ladoos*. On the Elephant God's birthday, called *Ganesh Chaturthi,* Indian women prepare a great feast in his honor. On that day, while the women are preparing the food, the men and children build a mud *Ganesh* and decorate him with colorful costumes and ornaments. Then the *ladoos* are symbolically offered to Ganesh as a *bhog* or sacrifice. In the evening all the people of the village gather together and take the mud Ganesh down to a river, in a gay, colorful procession which includes much singing and dancing. At the river's edge, the procession stops and Ganesh is taken to the deep-est part of the water and dropped in, to symbolize his *samadhi,* his disappearance into eternity. The children excitedly bid the Elephant God goodby and ask him to return early next year. The people then return to their homes, eager to begin their feast, which has *ladoos* as the main course.

Ladoos literally mean sweet balls. They can be prepared from *besan* (chick-pea flour), nut meal or from whole wheat flour. In the part of India where I was brought up, *ladoos* are traditionally made from wheat flour and are made especially for holidays such as *Ganesh Chaturthi.*

You will notice that the list of ingredients calls for the use of *ghee* or clarified butter in two different places. The second listing is for deep frying the *ladoos.* If you want, you can use a vegetable shortening like Crisco instead of *ghee.* This will reduce the cost of the preparation and I have found that it does an adequate job. Shortening cannot be substituted, however, for the first 3/4 cup of *ghee* listed.

In a wooden bowl, mix together the flour, cream of wheat and 1/4 cup melted, but not hot, *ghee.* Mix by rubbing the flour and *ghee* between your fingers. Now add the 4 tablespoons of water and using both hands, knead the ingredients into a very stiff dough. Continue to knead for 10 minutes and then gather together in a single mound. Divide the dough into as many egg-sized pieces as can be broken off. Now squeeze each of the pieces within your clenched fist, to form a sort of oblong-shaped piece of dough. Set aside all these oblong pieces of dough on a plate.

In a wok or heavy, shallow pot, heat the *ghee* or Crisco over a low flame. Test the liquid by dropping a bit of dough in the pot or wok. If the dough quickly bubbles and rises to the surface, then the shortening is ready for deep frying. Take 1 or 2 of the oblong pieces of dough and carefully place it in the hot *ghee* or oil. Cook the dough for 8 to 10 minutes, turning it around, from time to time, with a long-handled spoon. When the piece of dough has turned a reddish brown on all sides, remove with a slotted spoon and place on a layer of paper towels. Cook each piece of dough in this manner until all the pieces have been deep fried. Allow to cool for a few minutes so that they can be picked up with your hands. Then break each piece into 3 equal-size pieces.

The insides of the broken pieces of dough will be steaming hot, so allow them to cool for a few more minutes. When they can be easily handled, take a piece and crumble as finely as possible by rubbing between the palms of your hands. Crumble all the pieces in this manner until you have reduced the cooked dough to a pile of very fine crumbs. Next, using a strainer with a medium-to-large mesh, strain the crumbs by pushing them through with the tips of your fingers into a bowl.

Discard any of the larger pieces that will not go through the strainer. Sometimes the larger pieces can be further broken up by rolling them under a rolling pin and then straining them again.

Break open the cardamom pods and collect the small black seeds that are within. Crush these seeds very finely with a rolling pin and add them to the bowl of fine dough crumbs. Mix in the sugar and thoroughly stir all the ingredients together. Now pour 1/2 cup melted *ghee* or clarified butter (warm but not hot) into the dough mixture. Mix the ingredients thoroughly with your fingers until the dough becomes moist and begins to bind together into lumps. Take about 1/2 cup of the moist dough and form into a ball using the hollow of your palms. Your hands should be well covered with a layer of warm *ghee*, which gives the *ladoos* a smooth, shiny coating. When forming the *ladoos*, use a firm pressure, so that the dough is well compacted. The finished *ladoos* should be about the size of a large lemon. In India the *ladoos* are decorated by sprinkling small, white, *khuskhus* seeds over the top. These *khuskhus* seeds can be purchased in some Indian food stores but are purely for decoration and do not alter the taste. Serve these *ladoos* warm or cold, with other food or just by themselves.

Makes Six to Eight Ladoos

Sweets

SESAME CHIKKIS
(SWEET SESAME SEED TREATS)

1 cup sesame seeds
4 tablespoons melted ghee* or clarified butter
1/4 cup whole wheat flour
1/2 cup dark brown sugar
2 tablespoons water

*see glossary

This recipe comes from the beautiful beaches of Goa, on the western coast of India. During the time that I stayed in Goa, a little girl would pass on the beach in front of my house, selling *chikkis* that her mother had made. I quickly became an eager customer of this little girl who ran swiftly across the sand, carrying her jar of sesame *chikkis*. I finally convinced the girl to ask her mother for the recipe and on the day that I was to leave Goa, the girl came to my home and presented me with her mother's recipe.

A wok is the perfect cooking utensil for making *chikkis*, although any frying pan will do. Roast the sesame seeds in a wok or frying pan over a very low flame for about 5 minutes, stirring rapidly with a wooden spoon to prevent the delicate seeds from burning. When the seeds begin to redden, immediately empty them onto a plate.

Wipe off the pan with a towel, and in it heat 1 tablespoon of melted *ghee* or clarified butter over a low flame. Stir in the whole wheat flour and continue to stir the flour and *ghee* mixture for 3 to 5 minutes, until the flour reddens but does not burn. Now empty this flour into a clean bowl and again wipe the pan clean.

Add the remaining 3 tablespoons melted *ghee* or clarified butter to the wok along with the brown sugar. Turn the temperature to low and cook the ingredients for a minute while stirring with your wooden spoon. Now add the 2 tablespoons of water to the pan and continue to stir for another 2 or 3 minutes, until the ingredients blend into thick syrup. Then add the partially cooked flour and the roasted sesame seeds. Begin stirring all the ingredients together with a continual, steady motion. Cook and stir for approximately 5 minutes until a single, thick mass is formed. Transfer the thickened mixture from the frying pan to a clean plate.

When the *chikki* mixture has cooled down enough so that it can be handled, divide it into 9 or 10 equal-size pieces. Take each piece and roll into a ball using the palms of your hands. Each of the *chikkis* should be about the size of a lemon. Arrange them on a plate and let them cool to room temperature before serving. These *chikkis* can be eaten any time by themselves or served with tea. They will stay fresh for weeks when stored in a jar with a tight-fitting lid.
Makes Eight to Ten Chikkis

Sweets

BESAN BARFI
(SWEET CHICK-PEA SQUARES)

6 cardamom pods
3 tablespoons pistachios
5 tablespoons brown sugar
3 tablespoons water
4 tablespoons melted ghee* or clarified butter
1 cup besan* (chick-pea flour)

*see glossary

Lightly coat a serving dish with a layer of *ghee* and set aside. Break open the cardamom pods and remove all the small seeds. Discard the shells, collect the seeds and crush them very finely under a rolling pin. Now grind the unsalted pistachio nuts into a coarse meal with a rolling pin, and set these aside also.

In a small pot, combine the sugar and 3 tablespoons of water over a low heat and stir for 5 to 8 minutes. Turn the heat off when the mixture forms a syrup and begins to simmer. Leave the pot on top of the stove with the heat off so that the mixture stays warm.

In a heavy frying pan heat the melted *ghee* over a low temperature for 2 minutes. Now slowly add the *besan,* stirring continually with a wooden spoon. When all the *besan* has been added, sauté the mixture for 5 minutes, still over a low heat. After this, add the chopped pistachio nuts and continue to stir the mixture with a constant, steady motion for 10 to 15 minutes. Keep a close eye on the color of the *besan.* When it turns a light, reddish brown, add the crushed cardamom and warm sugar syrup. It is important that you continue stirring while you add the cardamom seeds and syrup. Continue to cook and stir the mixture for a few minutes until the syrup and *besan* blend together to form a thick, stiff mass. Quickly transfer this thickened mixture to the greased plate and spread it into a large circle with the back of a spoon. Spread the *barfi* evenly until it is within an inch from the edge of the dish. When the top surface of the *barfi* is cool enough to touch, use the palm of your hand to flatten and smooth the surface. Place this dish in a refrigerator for 1/2 hour so that it hardens enough to be cut. Then cut it into 2-inch squares and remove from the plate with a metal spatula. Serve *besan barfi* as a snack, with tea or as a dessert.

Serves Six

BADAM BARFI (ALMOND FUDGE)

3/4 cup whole, shelled almonds
or 1 cup chopped almonds
2 tablespoons shelled, unsalted pistachios
6 whole cardamom pods
1 cup milk
6 tablespoons honey or sugar
3 tablespoons melted ghee* or clarified butter

*see glossary

Soak the whole shelled almonds in a cup of luke-warm water for 1/2 hour. Pour off the water and remove the outer brown skin by scraping it off with your fingernail. Remove the shells from the unsalted pistachios and chop them into small pieces with a knife or crush them under a rolling pin. Set the nuts aside. Break the cardamom pods open and remove the small black seeds inside. Discard the outer pods, and crush the seeds as finely as possible by grinding them under a rolling pin. Now coat a pie plate with a light layer of *ghee* and put aside until needed.

Place the milk and the skinned almonds in an electric blender and blend until the almonds are well ground up. Add this almond milk to a small, heavy saucepot and cook over low-to-medium heat for 10 minutes, stirring constantly with a wooden spoon. Then add the honey or sugar and the chopped pistachios. Continue to stir until the honey is thoroughly blended in; then reduce the heat to low. Stir with a constant, steady motion and add the 3 tablespoons *ghee* or clarified butter. Cook and stir the mixture for 15 to 20 minutes until it forms a thick, lumpy consistency. Do not stop your stirring motion for even a moment, as this will cause the mixture to stick to the bottom. When the mixture reaches the thick, lumpy state, add the crushed cardamom seeds and stir thoroughly. Remove the pot from the heat.

Empty the thick fudge onto a pie plate or dish which has been coated with a light layer of *ghee*. Spread the fudge evenly over the plate with a spatula and let it cool off for awhile. When the fudge is cool enough to touch with your hands, spread a little *ghee* over your palm and pat the fudge down to spread it evenly and smoothly over the surface of the plate. Put the plate in the refrigerator for 1/2 hour so that it becomes hardened and completely cooled. Then cut the *barfi* into small squares or diamonds. Using a metal spatula, carefully lift the cut pieces from the plate and rearrange on another plate before serving.

These sweets can also be stored for a number of weeks when kept in a jar inside a refrigerator. Even when not refrigerated, they will keep for a number of days. In India these sweets are usually prepared in advance for some holiday and are given to children as a special treat.

Serves Six

Sweets

GULAB-JAMUN

1 cup instant, non-fat, dry milk
1/4 cup white, unbleached, all-purpose flour
2 pinches baking soda
3 tablespoons melted ghee* or clarified butter
3 to 4 tablespoons milk
1 cup light brown sugar
3 cups water
7 cardamom pods
1-1/2 to 1 cup ghee*
or Crisco for deep frying
1 teaspoon rose water

*see glossary

Gulab-jamuns are soft, sponge-like, brown, sweet balls that float around in a thick, flavored syrup. These sweets have a melt-in-your-mouth quality and despite the lengthy list of ingredients, they are fairly easy to prepare.

In a large mixing bowl, combine the dry milk, flour, baking soda and 3 tablespoons melted *ghee* or clarified butter. (Do not add the melted *ghee* until it has cooled to room temperature.) Using both hands, rub the mixture between your fingers and palms, so that the *ghee* is evenly distributed. Now add the liquid milk to the combined ingredients, sprinkling over a wide area of the mixing bowl. Begin kneading the ingredients with your hands to form a very stiff dough. If the dough is not moist enough to form a smooth, stiff consistency, add up to a tablespoon of water, a teaspoon at a time. When the dough forms a solid mass, remove from the mixing bowl and using the palms of your hands, knead for another 5 minutes or so. By now you should have a tight, smooth ball of dough.

Break off a piece of dough about 1-1/2 teaspoonfuls in size and roll it between your palms into a compact ball. If the dough sticks to your hands and crumbles, rub some melted butter over your palms. Continue forming these balls until all dough is used and set aside.

To prepare the syrup, cook the brown sugar and the 3 cups of water in a medium-size pot for 1/2 hour over a low-to-medium temperature. Stir the sugar and water once as it begins to cook and do not cover the pot. When cooked turn off the heat.

While waiting for the sugar and water to cook, break open the cardamom pods and gather together the small black seeds that are contained within. Discard the outer shell of the cardamom pods and crush the seeds under a rolling pin.

Add the 1-1/2 cups *ghee* or Crisco (vegetable shortening) to a small pot or wok. The wok needs less *ghee* or shortening than the pot. The Crisco vegetable shortening is a less expensive deep-frying medium and is therefore preferred by some people. However, if you prefer to use butter for that added richness, be sure that it is thoroughly clarified into *ghee*.

Heat the *ghee* or shortening over a low flame for 10 minutes. Cook from 3 to 5 of the dough balls at a time in the hot *ghee* for 3 to 4 minutes, turning frequently with a slotted spoon, to insure that all sides are evenly cooked. When the balls turn an even shade of brown, remove them with a draining spoon and place them on a layer of paper towels to remove any of the excess frying liquid.

After all the dough balls have been deep fried, rekindle the flame under the pot of sugar water. Set the temperature to low and stir in the crushed cardamom seeds. As soon as the sugar water begins to simmer, add all the fried dough balls and let them cook in the simmering syrup for 10 to 15 minutes. You will notice that as the balls float around in the simmering syrup, they will swell and the syrup will thicken and turn a brown color. When it appears that the floating dough balls have absorbed as much syrup as they can, turn off the heat.

Remove the balls of *gulab jamun* with a slotted, draining spoon and place them in a large mixing bowl. Stir the rose water into the syrup and pour the mixture over the balls. Let the *gulab jamun* cool at room temperature for about an hour, or put the bowl in the refrigerator for half an hour. When the *gulab jamun* is served, a few of the balls should be placed in a small dish along with some of the syrup.

Makes about Twenty Balls

Indian Meals and Feasts

An Indian meal, when properly prepared, will be appetizing, nutritionally balanced, and will offer enough variety in taste and flavors to satisfy even the most discriminating eater. A well-planned vegetarian diet can help an individual develop a healthy body and an alert mind. Unlike many of the vegetarian preparations of the West, Indian vegetarian cuisine is not meant to be a substitute for meat, nor is it meant to allay the desire for meat. Rather, the Indian vegetarian cuisine has a taste and appearance that is distinct among all the different styles of food preparation around the world.

A complete Indian meal, whether simply prepared for a daily menu or more elaborately cooked for some special occasion, will consist of these six basic and traditional items: *dal* (split lentil), rice, vegetable, *roti* (bread), yogurt and chutney. This is not to say, however, that all Indian meals must strictly adhere to this formula. The addition of a fresh fruit, or the deleting of one of the items is most common in India. In fact an abbreviated meal can be made from two or three of the items, but this would not be considered a complete meal in the traditional sense.

An Indian meal is served in individual, large, high-lipped, metal serving dishes known as *thalis*. Both the rice and bread are served in the *thali*, while the *dal*, vegetable and yogurt are served in small, separate metal bowls that are placed around the *thali*. The chutney, which is served in very small amounts, is placed near the inner edge of the metal *thali* lip. All the food is eaten and mixed in the *thali*, which acts as the counterpart of the plate and the bowl combined. These dishes are usually made from bright, yellow brass, which is one of the less expensive metals in India. In more recent times, the dishes have been made from stainless steel. In both cases they are brought to a high polish so that they seem almost to sparkle. Even when not being used, the gleaming dishes are placed on display in the kitchen, to act as decoration.

It is traditional that no beverage other than water or milk be served with the meal. However, a freshly brewed cup of *chai* (Indian milk tea) always follows the meal. In India, at the end of a meal, many people will chew *sopari* or *paan*, both betel nut preparations which are supposed to aid digestion and cleanse the mouth.

In South India the use of large banana leaves as a serving plate is quite popular. The banana leaf is used only once and each person receives a fresh leaf with the different food items spread in a particular pattern. The nicest part of using banana leaves is that there are no dishes to clean after the meal is finished.

Another difference between the traditional meal of South India and the traditional meal of Northern India is that the *rotis,* the different whole wheat breads, are rarely prepared in the South, because very little wheat is grown there. Instead, a flour made from rice and the *urad* lentil is used for certain bread-like preparations. They are, most notably, a soft, sponge-like cake known as *idli,* and a delicious, flat, spicy pancake, called *dosa.*

For a quickly prepared meal such as a lunch, or

Meals

when there is not enough time for a more complete menu, you can prepare a meal of a vegetable dish and rice or a vegetable dish and a bread. For an even briefer meal, you can prepare one of the many kinds of snacks and serve it with a chutney and some yogurt.

Breakfast is the simplest meal in India, usually consisting of *chai* (tea) and *thundi chapatis* (cold bread leftovers from the evening meal). In Southern India, however, more elaborate breakfasts are prepared, sometimes with freshly made rice-flour cakes or *dosa,* served with a spicy *sambhar* and some Indian-grown coffee.

Of the six traditional items that go to make up an Indian meal, each can be varied almost every day. This is one of the beauties of Indian vegetarian cooking. The different variations and combinations of dishes depend solely on the imagination of the cook and the availability of the different seasonal items. The many *dals* are available year round in the West (except for an occasional dock strike) and can be prepared in a variety of different ways. Even the traditional plain yogurt can be varied with the substitution of a *raita,* which is a mixture of plain yogurt, raw vegetables or fruits and some spices. In place of a chutney, a *cachumber* or Indian salad can be prepared. Although the use of fresh fruits and nuts is reserved for special meals and feasts in India, here in the West they can be served with almost every meal. So you see there is almost no end to the variety in the Indian vegetarian cuisine. Western explorers risked their lives and fortunes searching for the fabled spices of the East. Now with much less effort you can rediscover some of the culinary joys of India.

PREPARING FOR A FEAST

A feast in India is actually a celebration of life. No matter what the cause of the celebration, a religious holiday, a wedding, an engagement party or even a grandfather's funeral, the people devote their entire energies and resources to making the celebration as joyous as possible. Indian people work very hard and they take their moments of celebration very seriously, so that little, if anything, is spared for the occasion. All the houses are meticulously cleaned, especially the kitchens, which receive a new floor covering made from cow dung. This may sound like a very unhygienic practice but actually quite the opposite is true. When the dung dries it is odorless and free of any bacteria; it also makes a durable and practical floor covering.

The dishes that will be prepared for a feast or holiday are quite different from the meals that are served on ordinary days. First, the traditional six items are considered insufficient and as many as 15 to 20 separate dishes will be prepared. Secondly only the highest quality of food will be used, the best rice available, the finest and most costly *dals* and only the purest *ghee.* And lastly at least one sweet dish is prepared to be eaten with the meal. I think it is the inclusion of this sweet dish that most sets apart the festive menu from the daily menu.

Since the sweet dish is so highly regarded and so important to the gaiety of a feast, it will be the most important item prepared. Possibly at the end of the meal a selection of fresh fruits such as mangos or papayas will be served, if the cost is not beyond the means of the people preparing the feast.

At least two vegetable dishes should be served at a feast. One a dry vegetable (without sauce) and the other a vegetable with a sauce. (See the chapter on vegetable dishes to get a fuller explanation of dry and "wet" vegetable dishes.) A special, fancy bread such as *puris* or *parothas* will be made for the feast instead of the more ordinary *rotis.* In addition to the specially prepared breads, a *papad* will be either roasted or deep fried. Certainly a more expensive, finer grade of rice will be served, such as *basmati* rice. Or a colorful rice *pilau* will be prepared in place of the standard plain rice. And there will always be at least one appetizer such as *samosa* or *batata vada,* served piping hot with a freshly prepared chutney, to stimulate one's appetite for the great meal ahead. Here is a sample menu of what might be prepared for an Indian feast. All the ingredients are available in local Indian stores or through one of the mail-order emporiums listed in the back of the book.

Feasts

MENU FOR A SPECIAL FEAST

Bhajia (For an Appetizer), Page 30
Shrikhand, Page 63
Puris, Page 156
Cauliflower and Peas (Dry Vegetable), Page 89
Eggplant and Potatoes (Vegetable in Sauce), Page 71
Basmati Rice, Page 103, or
Rice with Raisins and Nuts, Page 107
Toor Dal, Page 122
Papadam, Page 159
Cachumber, Page 53
Preserved Mango Chutney, Page 47
Coconut Chutney, Page 51, or
Mint Chutney, Page 49
A Fresh Tropical Fruit
(Mango, Papaya, Pineapple)
Chai (Prepared with
Darjeeling Tea), Page 19

Veg w/ Sauce P 80
Dry veg   P. 86
Chise/Peas P.58
Rice w/ Nuts Rasins 107
toor dal P 122
Cachumber P 53
yogurt
Raisin Chutney P. 50
cuke Raita   P.52
Fruit, Chai

Although this list seems quite extensive, it is within the range of any Western cook, even one who has never before cooked an Indian meal. The only item that is not generally available in the West, that usually appears at the end of an Indian feast, is *paan*. This betel-nut preparation served at the end of a special meal is prepared by professionals in India. They blend together their secret herbs and spices along with the betel nut, which, when taken after a meal, is supposed to intensify one's feelings of satisfaction and also aid the digestive process.

If you are going to arrange an Indian feast such as the one just described, try to plan it some days in advance. It is extremely helpful if you can get a friend or relative to help you, especially if you are going to cook for more than six people. However, it is not good to have too many people in the kitchen, because as they say, "too many cooks spoil the *dal*." Try to plan out the amount of time you will need as well as planning what ingredients and utensils will be necessary. Read through the recipes a few times before you actually begin to cook. You should realize that the more people you cook for, the more time you will need to prepare some of the items.

Plan out the sequence of which dishes will be cooked first, second and so on. For example, almost all Indian sweets can be cooked a day in advance, and stored in the refrigerator until needed. Also, the fresh chutney, *raita* or *cachumber* (salad) can be prepared many hours in advance on the day the meal is to be served. The *dal* should be one of the first things to be prepared, as it generally takes the longest cooking time and can easily be reheated just prior to being served. While the *dal* is cooking, begin washing and cutting up the vegetables, or delegate this job to the person who may be helping you. The preparation of the vegetables, while requiring little special knowledge, will often be more time-consuming than the actual cooking. The last items to be cooked should be the breads and appetizers, since it is very important that they be as freshly cooked as possible when served. For these last two items, a helping hand is most beneficial. You can prepare the dough for the breads and the person who is helping can roast or deep fry them while you attend to something else. Or if you are preparing *bhajias* for an appetizer, you can prepare the batter and the person helping you can deep fry the different vegetables. In this way you will be able to coordinate the cooking of the different items and still be assured of their freshness.

In India, meals are generally eaten on the floor, with the participants sitting, with their legs crossed, in front of their food. For a special meal the eating area should be decorated with some flowers and the air can be flavored with some mild, pleasant incense. The dishes should be arranged so as to add to the festiveness of the occasion. Be a little creative in setting up the eating area so that even upon sitting down, your guests' appetites will be stimulated. Now is the time that the *dal* and vegetable dishes should be reheated, if they are not already hot.

Feasts

Indian food is meant to be eaten with your hands. In India only the right hand is used; the left hand is considered unclean because it is used for certain cleansing functions. There are no set rules for the proper way to eat with your hands. The best advice is to eat in a way that is natural and comfortable. If a bread, such as *chapatis* are served, pieces can be broken off and used to gather some of the food together. With the piece of *chapati* wrapped around some vegetables or rice, you can make a little "sandwich" to pop in your mouth. In some parts of India it is customary to mix the vegetables, rice and yogurt together with your fingers in the process of eating. Whether you use your hands or a fork and spoon, eat in a way that tastes and feels best to you.

Just before eating, a short *sloka* or prayer will be said in honor of the occasion. And then a piece of the food is thrown into the fire as an offering to the God of Fire, Agni, in the hope that His greatness, which is responsible for such feasts, will bring about many more celebrations.

Where to Buy
Indian Spices and Dry Goods

WEST

*Bazaar of India, 1331 University Avenue,
   Berkeley, California 94702
*Bezjian's Grocery, 4725 Santa Monica Blvd.,
   Los Angeles, California 90029
 California Direct Import Co. (Oh's), 2651 Mission St.,
   San Francisco, California 94110
*Haig's Delicacies, 642 Clement St., San Francisco,
   California 94118
*India Imports & Exports, 10641 West Pico Blvd.,
   Los Angeles, California 90064
*Porter's Food Unlimited, 125 West 11th St.,
   Eugene, Oregon 97401
*Specialty Spice Shop; mail order address: 2757 152nd
   Avenue, N.E., Redmond, Washington 98052; retail
   outlet: Pike Place Market, Seattle, Washington 98101
*Tarver's Delicacies, De Anza Shopping Center,
   1338 South Mary Avenue, Sunnyvale,
   California 94087
 Wholy Foods, 2999 Shattuck Avenue, Berkeley,
   California 94705

MIDWEST

*India Gift and Food Store, 1031 Belmont,
   Chicago, Illinois 60657
*International House of Foods, 440 West Gorham St.,
   Madison, Wisconsin 53703

SOUTH

*Antone's, 2606 South Sheridan, Tulsa,
   Oklahoma 74129
*Jay Store, 4023 Westheimer, Houston, Texas 77027
 Jung's Oriental Foods and Gifts,
   2519 North Fitzburgh, Dallas, Texas 75204
 Yoga and Health Center, 2912 Oaklawn,
   Dallas, Texas 75222

EAST

*Aphrodisia, 28 Carmine St., New York,
   New York 10014
*House of Spices, 76-17 Broadway,
   Jackson Heights, New York 11373
*India Food and Gourmet, 110 Lexington Ave.,
   New York, New York 10016
*Indian Super Bazaar; mail order address: P.O. Box 1977,
   Silver Spring, Maryland 20902; retail outlets:
   3735 Rhode Island, Mt. Rainier, 20822; International
   Bazaar, 7720 Wisconsin Avenue, Bethesda, 20014
*Kalpana Indian Groceries, 4275 Main St.,
   Flushing, New York 11355
*K. Kalustyan, Orient Export Trading Corp.,
   123 Lexington Ave., New York, New York 10016
 T. G. Koryn, Inc., 66 Broad St.,
   Carlstad, New Jersey 07072
*Spice Corner, 904 South 9th,
   Philadelphia, Pennsylvania 19147
*Spices and Foods Unlimited, Inc., 2018 A Florida Ave.,
   N.W., Washington D.C. 20009

CANADA

*T. Eaton's Co., 190 Yonge St., Toronto 205, Ontario
*S. Enkin Inc., Imports and Exports,
   1201 St. Lawrence, Montreal 18, Quebec

*these will mail order

Glossary

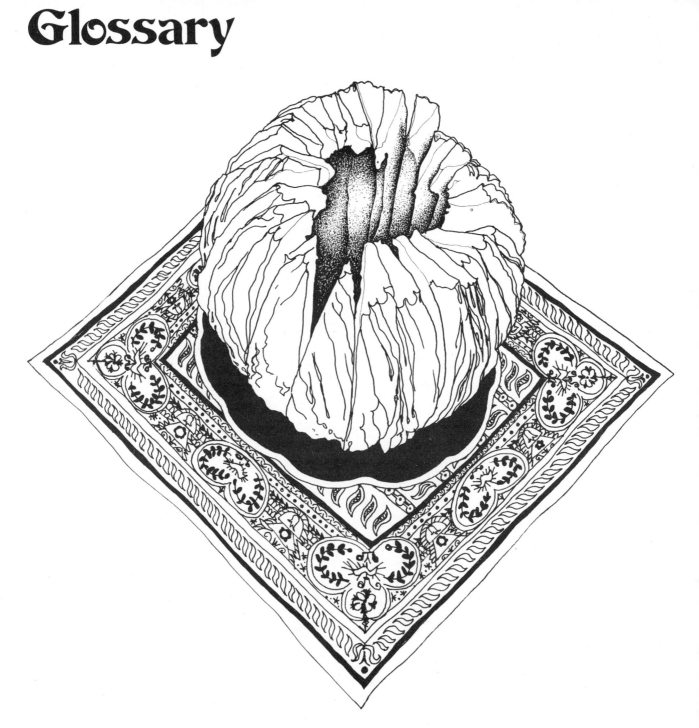

Glossary

ADU Fresh ginger root, page 11
ALU or BATATA Potato
ASAFETIDA Hing, page 10
BARFI Sweet nut squares,
    pages 174-175
BASMATI RICE An aromatic rice
    grown in North India, pages 99, 103
BATATA or ALU Potato
BESAN Chick-pea flour or garbanzo
    bean flour, page 13
BHAJI or SHAK Cooked vegetables,
    page 69
BHAJIA or PAKORA Vegetables
    deep-fried in batter, page 30
BHAKARIS Thick Indian bread,
    page 149
BHANG Marijuana drink served
    cool, pages 26-27
BOTTLE GOURD Ghiya, page 67
CHAI Tea, page 17-18
CHANA Chick-pea, page 121
CHANA DAL Split chick-pea,
    page 124
CHAPATI or ROTI Unleavened
    Indian bread, pages 15, 144
CHAVAL or BHAT Rice
CHHASH Milk by-product or thin
    buttermilk, page 55
CHIVRA A crunchy muncher, page 45
CORIANDER LEAVES Cilantro,
    Chinese parsley or Mexican
    parsley, page 10
DAHI Yogurt or curd, pages 60-63
DAL Split grain or lentil,
    pages 14, 121-122
DHANIA Coriander, page 10
DOODH Milk, page 22
DOODHI Ghiya or opo, see
    also bottle gourd, 67
DOSA Spicy pancake, page 42
FARASAN Snacks, page 29
GALKA Zucchini-like vegetable,
    page 68

GARAM MASALA Ground mixture
    of certain hot Indian spices,
    page 13
GHEE Indian clarified butter, page 14
GHEESODA Ghiya-like vegetable, or
    Chinese opo, page 68
GHIYA Indian squash or opo, page 67
GULAB JAL Rose water, page 11
GUR Raw unbleached cane sugar,
    page 161
HALDI Turmeric, page 12
HING Asafetida, page 10
IDLI Spicy steamed cake
ILAICHI Cardamom pod, page 10
IMLI Tamarind, page 12
JAIFAL Nutmeg, page 11
JARA Slotted metal spoon, page 15
JEERA Cumin, page 11
KADHAI Indian cooking utensil
    similar to the Japanese wok,
    page 15
KADHI Yogurt soup, page 62
KARELA Green squash variety with
    a slightly bitter taste, page 68
KESAR Saffron, page 12
KHEER Indian-style rice pudding
KHICHADI or KHICHARI Rice
    cooked with dal, page 113
KHUSKHUS SEEDS Small white
    poppy seeds, page 17
KOFTA Grated vegetable balls
    cooked with chick-pea flour,
    page 76
LADOO Sweet ball, page 170
LASAN Garlic, page 11
LASSI Yogurt or buttermilk
    drink, pages 22, 23
LAVING Cloves, page 10
MARI Black or white pepper, page 11
MASOOR DAL Small split lentil,
    pages 14, 122, 127
METHI Fenugreek seeds, page 11
MIRCHI Cayenne pepper, page 10

Glossary

MOTH or MUTH Small brown lentil, page 14

MUNG or MOONG Small green bean, page 138

MUNG DAL Split mung bean, pages 14, 125

MUSTARD POWDER (BLACK) Ground black mustard seeds. Dry English mustard may be sutstituted but a lesser amount should be used, pages 11, 52

NALIAR Coconut, page 111

OPO Ghiya, page 67

PAAN Leaf from the Nagarvel tree. Preparation of paan is made by folding the leaf around certain spices and sopari (betel nut).

PAKORA or BHAJIA Deep-fried vegetables in batter, page 30

PANIR Indian homemade cheese, pages 56, 57

PAPAD or PAPADAM An Indian crisp or chip, page 159

PAROTHA Multi-layered Indian bread, page 150

PATLI Rolling board, page 15

PHODINO Mint, page 11

PURIS Puffed breads, page 156

RAI Black mustard seeds, page 11

RAITA Yogurt dip or salad with a yogurt base, page 52

RASEDAR SHAK Vegetables with sauce, page 71

ROTI or CHAPATI Unleavened Indian bread, pages 15, 144

SAMOSA Vegetable rolls, page 40

SEV Spicy noodle, page 38

SHAK Cooked vegetables

SOPARI Bitter, pungent nut resembling a nutmeg. Placed inside the paan leaf to make the paan preparation, page 179

SUBJI or BHAJI Cooked vegetables, page 69

SUKI BHAJI Dry vegetable dish, page 69

TAJ Cinnamon, page 10

TAMARIND or IMLI Pod-filled sweet and sour fruit, page 12

THALI Individual metal serving dish, pages 61, 179. See illustration, page 154

TOOR DAL Split yellow peas or pigeon peas, page 123

WOK Japanese deep frying utensil similar to the Indian kadhai, page 15

URAD or UDUD Small black lentil, white when skinned, page 126

URAD DAL Split urad lentil, pages 122, 126

VADHAR The sautéing process in oil, page 69

VELAN Rolling pin, page 15

Index

Index

Index

Biographical Notes

SHANTA NIMBARK SACHAROFF

Shanta Sacharoff was born in the town of Bhoringada in the state of Gujarat in the northwest of India. Like most Indian girls, she learned to cook at an early age and much of her youth was spent in her family's kitchen. She attended the Home School in Bhavnagar and in 1964 came to the United States to attend Russell Sage College in Troy, New York. She graduated from Adelphi College in Long Island with a degree in psychology. After graduation she traveled through Europe and Asia and became acquainted with various vegetarian cuisines of the different nations. In 1969 Shanta returned to India with her future husband, Stanley Sacharoff, where they were married and lived for awhile. Shanta presently lives in the San Francisco Bay Area where her husband is a counselor at the California School for the Deaf in Berkeley. Shanta teaches Indian cooking, has given cooking demonstrations on educational television and is the author of several magazine articles on food.

LINDA ROBERTSON

Linda Robertson has a degree in fine arts from Washington University in St. Louis. Married to a physician, she has lived in San Francisco for many years and worked as an art director, free-lance graphic designer and artist. She also illustrated "Herb Cookery" for 101 Productions.